FOND RECOLLECTIONS OF CAPTIVITY

An Austrian POW in Wales

Studies in Austrian Literature, Culture, and Language

Translation Series

FOND RECOLLECTIONS OF CAPTIVITY

An Austrian POW in Wales

by Horst Jarka

"Perhaps one day you will even wish you could relive these days"

> From a letter my mother in Austria wrote to me at Ruperra Castle,
> Branch of POW Camp 197, Chepstow
> May 22, 1946

Ariadne Press
Riverside, California
&
University of Montana Press
Missoula, Montana

Library of Congress Cataloging-in-Publication Data

Jarka, Horst, author.
Fond recollections of captivity : an Austrian POW in Wales / by Horst Jarka.
Other titles: Austrian POW in Wales
Riverside, California : Ariadne Press, [2017] | Series: Studies in Austrian literature, culture, and language translation series |
Includes bibliographical references and index.

LCCN 2017028387 | ISBN 9781572412089 (pbk. " alk. paper)
LCSH: Jarka, Horst. | World War, 1939-1945--Prisoners and prisons, British. | World War, 1939-1945--Wales.| Prisoners of war--Wales Biography.|Prisoners-of-war--Germany--Biography. | Germany. Heer Officers--Biography. | World Ware, 1939-1945 Personal narratives, Austrian. | Prisoners of war--Aystrua--Biography. | Vienna (Auustria)--Biography.
LCC D805.G7 J37 2017 | DDC 940.54/72429092 [B] --dc23
LC record available at https://lccn..loc.gov/2017028387

Cover
Designer: Neal Wiegert

Copyright 2017
by Ariadne Press
270 Goins Court
Riverside, CA 92507

All right reserved.
No part of this publication may be transmitted in any form or by any means without formal permission.
Printed in the United States of America
ISBN 978-1-57241-208-9

In affectionate memory of

William J. B. Rees
Mary Rees
Vivian Jones
Ernie Oram

Acknowledgments

My warmest thanks to Gerald A. Fetz, Emeritus Professor of German and Dean of the University of Montana's College of Arts and Sciences, my valued colleague of many years, and my friend. In his enthusiasm for my memoirs, he has been the inspiration behind the sometimes tedious editorial and technical work of preparing my manuscript for print. As Director of the University of Montana Press, he has had the invaluable help of Neal Wiegert, designer of the evocative cover of this volume, and Ken Price, Director of the Press' Printing and Graphics Unit, who was responsible for the remarkably clear reproduction of the old photos and documents. I want to thank especially as well Jorun and Karl Johns of Ariadne Press in Riverside, California for their most generous cooperation with the UM Press to make this publication possible.

CONTENTS

Preface 1
Becoming a Soldier 2
To the "Front" 10
"Vee Vant to Surrrender!" 16
POW Camps—Belgium, Enghien 20
Jabekke 22
England Camp 17—Sheffield 25
Camp 189—Dunham Park 33
Wales Camp 197—Chepstow 34
Mobile Field Bakery—Ruperra Castle 38
England Camp 685 102
Long Marston 106
Camp 23—Sudbury 108
Camp 186—Colchester 120
Camp 409—Aylsham 134
Austria 147
Back to Wales 168
...And Back Again 176
...And Again 180
Epilogue/Greenmeadow Now 183
Sketches and Letters 186
Afterword 197

PREFACE

I was a POW in Wales for one year. That year was very special to me and proved to be of importance in my whole life. I am now seventy-five. The second World War is history, and memory is elusive. But I am fortunate in having kept a diary of my POW time. Journals are problematic, however, and my POW one especially so, for humorously ironic reasons. As a young man of twenty with Romantic notions of my self-importance, I lived under the illusion that my journal might be read by the camp officer. After all, it had been taken away from me at one of the searches and was returned to me (read or unread) several weeks later and only after my having requested that it be returned. My suspicions probably were completely unfounded; still, I wrote in my POW-journal only things that could pass English military eyes. The same is true of the letters I wrote, many of which I still have. I also have all of the letters I received; of these, the ones from Austria were also censored. The letters were an essential part of my life as a POW, and I have incorporated many in my account. But journal and letters don't tell the whole story.

What made my year in Wales so special was my "secret" life which was only hinted at in what I wrote down, but is indelibly impressed on my memory, which is more telling than my handwriting. To tell the whole story I will tell both stories at the same time. I will translate my German diary and quote from the letters, and then interpolate what my memory still holds. To differentiate between the levels, the journal will be in italics, the letters indented, and the remembered additions in regular font. There had to be another level, another time level as well. Some journal entries made me ask: did I really write this? And some of what I remember but never wrote down evokes the same sobering realization of how much I was still thinking in manipulated patterns of propaganda. At least an attempt to explain, not to excuse, seems necessary to me, or the whole endeavor would be reduced to an exercise in unreflected nostalgia.

One of the reasons for writing all this down is to show how my experience in Wales helped me on the way to overcoming these limitations. Not the least of these was my self-absorption. At a time when endless millions were suffering I, and I suspect many other POWs, was absorbed in what was often little more than an inconvenience. The words "barbed wire" alone could trigger a melodramatic self-pity which, in the light of the horrors of the holocaust, strike me now as downright immoral. But again, my time in Wales made me also realize how fortunate I was, and only when I was transferred to other camps was I pulled back into the POW-syndrome of feeling sorry for myself, a particularly phoney kind of self-indulgence at a time when we were on our way home.

I have written up all this for my children and grandchildren but also as a tribute to Wales and to the Welsh friends I made there, that is in the tiny corner on the border of Glamorgan and Monmouth (now Gwent) where I spent that year, and where, after my early exposure to destruction and hate, was gently led back to quiet and hope, human understanding and trust. Perhaps these words are too big for what happened. The process was "dramatic" and "romantic" only in the imagination of a boy of twenty, and today may be comprehensible only for young people who are not yet desensitized by sensationalism. How easy it is for young people nowadays to travel abroad, to meet people in different parts of the world!

Being in Wales as a prisoner of war–or rather a prisoner of peace, because when I, after a number of camps, ended up in Wales, the war was just about over—made me see the other side, the side of the "enemy," and I wanted to see more of it. In Wales I began reading English literature, and Welsh friends helped me then and long after I had started my study of English at the University of Vienna. I wrote my dissertation on Alun Lewis.

In order to bring out the significance which that year gained for me over time, I have to put it in its frame: I have to sketch what happened before and after I had seen action, during the months in the camps before, in, and after those in Wales, and the years after my return to Austria.

Becoming A Soldier

I graduated from the Gymnasium (college-bound High School) in my home town Klosterneuburg near Vienna in the spring of 1943, and was drafted into the German Army two weeks after my eighteenth birthday in August. I had not volunteered but was eager to prove my manliness, perhaps because I had grown up without a father. My basic training was that of Panzergrenadiers, actually, motorized infantry. Our specialty was to fight from those half-track personnel carriers which old soldiers appropriately called "coffins on wheels."

Our garrison was in Frydek-Mistek in Moravia, that is to say: we recruits

Horst Jarka, 18, in 1943

were part of the German army which occupied Czechoslovakia. It was little more than a year after Czech resistance fighters had assassinated Heydrich, one of the top SS-chiefs close to Himmler, and deputy of the German governor of Czechoslovakia; in retaliation the Germans had surrounded Lidice, the village near Prague, where supposedly the assassins had been hiding, shot nearly 200 men, deported the women to a concentration camp, and razed the village to the ground. In the autumn of 1943 the tension must have been considerable, but did not seem to surface too much; at least I don't remember being warned of the Czech population, probably because our area, on the edge of the Sudeten-District, was mixed. Frydek (Friedek) was mostly German and Mistek, its sister city, mostly Czech.

The journal I kept during that year of training gives only a very scanty record of the decisive events from the autumn of 1943 to the summer of 1944, and is even less revealing about my reactions. I was too tired to write much. There were drills, forced marches on which we had to sing under gasmasks and which usually ended with pedantic inspections of gear after sadistically short cleaning periods—the usual army routine that was supposed to make us into unthinking obedient cogs in the machine of war. There were manoeuvres in the autumn with campfires which revived my romanticism, and there were winter manoeuvres which had the opposite effect: I remember lying in the snow with my rifle frozen stiff like my fingers, and I was thinking: if the Russians were attacking now, I'd give up. Enthusiasm and fear were the two emotions which, to a varying degree, determined my reactions. My frequent but short letters home to mother and Ilse, my girlfriend, oozed with cheerfulness, not only because they were censored. They were ordinary soldiers' letters about packages received or lost, socks, underwear, and hopes of home leave.

    Dear Mother.   September 16, 1943

Yesterday I received your last two packages—a cause of great jubilation for the soul: *Faust*, and for the tummy: cookies. *Faust* is eternal, the cookies are not. They are already gone, since we don't get any sweets here.

****

Today I am going up a hill. The hills here are as high as the ones at home. Some are even higher!

Went to a movie last night. Odd to see the Czech subtitles while German is being spoken.

Sunday, October 17, 1943

Beautiful morning. Went to the woods and read. The forest here is cut through with pleasant paths which are not frequented. Thank God! I am glad when it's quiet. In the barracks it's always noisy.

Only in my journal would I occasionally acknowledge that it was getting harder to be cheerful all the time.

September 9, 1943

Today convocation of the Battalion. Italy has capitulated. The mood is not very confident. Everybody believes that our training is not going to last very long. In a few minutes rollcall for night manoeuvres.

September 10, 1943

At 20:15 the Führer's address to the German people. The company is called together in the garage to listen. Although it did not last very long, many were asleep. The interest in events of our time must be overwhelming indeed. Three names were taken.

At the end of the year some of us were sent home on front-leave. One of them gave me his picture for remembrance. It was one of those first pictures in uniform all of us sent home. But his was different; he had had it taken without the military cap. I still have it: an intelligent face with a critical, slightly amused look, almost a smirk, the face of a young intellectual more mature than most of us, like a civilian in a brand new army jacket. On the back he had written "Catch me please" in English and below that, in German: "Dein Freund und Kamerad Reinhold Docker (Ignaz)." I don't know what happened to him. Presumably he was sent to Russia, unless he was sent west, where his hope of surrendering would have been more likely to be fulfilled. Looking at his photo now, I see him as representing one of the alternatives of my generation. Reinhold saw through all the propaganda, saw the inevitable catastrophe and had decided not to be a hero nor a martyr, not to be taken in, and to survive as best he could. I was still caught up in the juvenile idealism of soldierdom patriotism and ambition. It just took me a little longer to come to Reinhold's conclusion. The officers must have sensed where Reinhold stood, and he obviously was not one of us to be transferred to the ROB-course (the equivalent to the British OCTU: Officer Cadets' Training Unit) at the beginning of the year. I was proud of being chosen, and mother was relieved because my transfer meant a delay of my frontline service and my survival till then. She had been a nurse in a field hospital in World War I and knew what war was like.

The OCTU was in the nearby town of Hranice (we used the German name Mährisch Weisskirchen), in the same barracks where cadets in the Austro-Hungarian Monarchy had been made into officers. Robert Musil had been there and had written about it in *Young Torless* (1906). I had never heard of Musil, nor did I experience in those barracks the intricate psychological trauma Musil described. Our training promised varied military expertise (as will become clear, in my case all that training proved to be a futile investment). We were trained to fire anti-tank guns and light infantry artillery, and panzerfausts. We learned to drive all kinds of trucks running on sickly smelling wood gas, we drove those "coffins on wheels," and of course tanks. I liked driving a tank through Czech villages avoiding flocks of geese (any number of fowl under four, however, was fair game, though I never hit any). We were even promised to learn to drive, in a pinch, steam locomotives but never got around to that boyhood dream. If it had not been for the shooting range, all this training, the new skills with all sorts of "machines," would have made us almost forget its sole purpose. And when the training NCOs, happy to be away from the front, talked about it, their advice and warnings often sounded to us more like their past than our future.

The future, however, could not be denied.

February 2, 1944

Driving school. Spent the day driving along the Slovak border. The landscape is beautiful up in the foothills of the Carpathian mountains which might as well be in Styria. We stopped for lunch in Bedschwa where Czech soldiers are billeted. How scornfully they looked at us. They must be jubilant now that things at the eastern front are getting worse every day. How is it all going to end? Yesterday Army Headquarters reported: Luzk lost. If things go on like that! But something must happen. It must not be that we doubt. Must not be? And yet everybody is downcast and pessimistic. –Russia. Land without end. Countless soldiers' graves cover you where German soldiers left long ago. More and more often one hears the question: what if..

Ilse has passed the High School finals and, on February 15th, will be drafted to the Women's Work Force to help on the farms.

Reinhold Döcker (Ignaz)

Inspite of these forebodings the business of the OCTU went on in almost peacetime fashion. Once on home leave I heard the rumbling of the flak and the detonations of the bombs in Vienna over the hills from my hometown. But here in Hranice we felt nothing of the war. We once took a field trip to one of the many coalmines in this economically so important area.

> Dear Mother,
> ...I gained insight into the miserable toil of these poor devils who break the coal out of the rock. For 6.50 Reichsmarks they are working 8 hours a day on their bellies; the seams are often not higher than 20 inches, and the miners sweat their humanity out of their bodies...All the more important it is to conserve on coal.

My social conscience blended with the public appeal for the war effort that screamed from posters all over the country.
We were taken to see a German production of Ibsen's *Ghosts* [!] in Morawa Ostrawa, the biggest town around, and there were dances with the German population. Once I danced with a shy Czech girl with big dreamy eyes and beautiful black braids. Neither spoke the other's language. We only smiled at each other, and she gave me her name. I never saw her again. On weekends I liked to go to a Czech tavern in the woods where the waiter took his time serving German soldiers, but the roasted goat was delicious.
The winter training especially had an unreal vacation atmosphere about it. We learned to crawl through snow drifts on white skis in white "nightgowns" that completely covered us and made skiing, if successful at all, a kind of ghoulish affair. I still have a snapshot of a Prussian officer who, shouting "A yes, a no, a straight line, a goal!" (supposedly a Nietzsche-quote) was determined to master Alpine skiing but, to our roaring delight, ended every run buried in a cloud of snow. This skiing holiday in the Slovak Carpathians ended, like all holidays, with a sobering return to reality.

March 16, 1944
Last evening in the hut. Today was a glorious day of sunshine on the sparkling slopes that we swooped down. Armed with a few words of Czech we started out for one of those solitary farms in the valley. Everything worked fine. The woman understood our "chlepa" and "mleko" right away and soon enough we could fortify ourselves with a mug of rich

milos and a wedge of bread. An odd family it was. Grandfather crawled up to the top of the stove to make room for us on the bench, the daughter rolled up the wool she had been spinning. The farmer was sorting the seed for sowing as was the man on the bench in the corner who looked not quite right in the head. The woman was cooking, and the youngest member of the family kept staring at us. Our various attempts at communication led nowhere. Only later did we get some idea of what the farmer was trying to tell us. We kept hearing the words "Bolschewiki," and "Tarnopol." He was well informed about what was happening at the front.

On their advance west the Red Army had just crossed the old Russian-Polish border and surrounded Tarnopol.

He smiled from ear to ear as he said, "Tarnopol–Morawa Ostrawa–Frydeck–Mistek–Hranice" naming the towns in Czechoslovakia which the Russians would soon reach on their seemingly inexorable advance west—the towns to which we would return after our skiing interlude. For the Slovak the war would be over as soon as the Russians came.

With full tummies we climb back up to the ridge. The brilliance of sun and snow—the sky, through the goggles, bluer than ever—all that makes one take a liberating breath of exhilaration, grateful to experience something so beautiful. But that, too, will pass. Tomorrow at this time we will be miles from here in Hranice, with nothing to look forward to but spring mud and the mad rush from one whistle of the corporal to the next.
I go outside. The magnificent starry sky.

Tarnopol was taken by the Russians four days later. The Slovak peasant had been right: the front was coming closer and closer. One day in the barracks I met Gustav Fischer, my classmate in Klosterneuburg, who had volunteered before our final exams and now went through Hranice on leave from the Eastern Front. While we were alone in the locker room, he quickly showed me snapshots illustrating what life, or rather death, on the front was like: pictures of mutilated faces, limbs torn from the body, bloated bodies with deep gashes, covered with blood. These pictures – for showing them to another soldier Gustav could possibly have been court-marshalled – made me recall the horror of war my mother had told me about so many times, and fear replaced all my romantic notions of soldiering, at least for a couple of days. The desire to prove myself and be brave returned, especially with my promotion to lance-corporal – but that one silver chevron could not quite outshine the anxiety that increased as the end of the OCTU-course came nearer. But now I did want to see action, preferably not on the Eastern Front, and I was not alone in that hope. In the back of my mind there was the possibility of being taken prisoner, and the Russians were reputed not to observe the Geneva Convention whereas the western allies were supposed to respect it. When we were loaded on the train after my last leave in August 1943 (I had celebrated my 19th birthday at home), and the train went to Munich and not to Czechoslovakia, we knew that we were supposed not to stop the Red Army but *only* the Americans and the British.

To The "Front"

We were to be assigned to various front-line units. But in August 1944 the front-line was not so easy to make out, and we spent a long time trying to find our units. In my memory those weeks are one blur of confusion. I have to rely almost completely on my journal and my short letters home. Mother must have got the impression that I led a life of carefree vagabondage which, considering what others went through, was not too far off the mark. A few snatches from my journal probably give a clearer picture of both my, and the general, mood among our group of OCTU-cadets than would the journal in its entirety.

August 15, 1944
Metz-Paris. The train stood most of the night. According to the engineer the engine wouldn't work; we suspected that he said this because the tracks from Metz to Paris are often strafed by the RAF. We just passed a burnt-out fuel train. When are they going to rake us with bullets? The best indication of their coming is that the train suddenly stops and the engineers who are French run off.

August 16, 1944
Yesterday afternoon we were under fire from the air. As soon as everybody rushed out of the train they shot at us from the ground. Gert and I, lying behind a bush, heard the bullets whistle. Partisans? We were included in a patrol which was sent off immediately–without ammunition. We hopped back on the moving train. We were moving slowly, at a walking pace through the uncanny dusk. If the partisans had been on the ball, we would never have reached Paris. Burning fuel trucks. Coming to a destroyed bridge we had to get out and,

while a thunderstorm was brewing behind us, cross the river on a makeshift wooden bridge. Pitch dark night. Only when lightning flared could we make out the outlines of what was left of the bridge. Bomb craters. More craters. In a tunnel on the other side a train was waiting for us. The seven of us found an excellent car with luxurious benches, one for each of us! We washed, and then I slept until Franz woke me up, and I saw that we were in Paris. 7:15 a.m.

Paris, August 17, 1944
Midnight. A day of sightseeing. In the morning we strolled along the boulevard in the rain. Notre Dame. To my pleasant surprise I communicate quite well with the Parisians. In the afternoon: Madeleine, Arch of Triumph, and the grave of the Unknown Soldier under it. Stroll down to the Eiffel Tower. Unfortunately it's already closed for the day, and we miss going up.

Like any tourist I bought postcards and sent a bunch home: glossy black-and-whites, hardly any cars in the streets. A glorious summer sky. I had written nothing on the back, except on one, the words "please keep." I still have them: Sacre-Coeur, Notre Dame, L'Arc de Triomphe, Eglise de la Madeleine, L'Obelisque des la Place de la Concorde, Le Palais de Chaillot, La Tour Eiffel. In 1940 German soldiers probably sent home the very same cards as proof of their triumph. In 1944 my cards were a souvenir of my illusion: one morning of playing peace in the midst of war. Today they are a ghostly reminder of a grotesquely unreal moment of arrested time.

22:00. We are back at the railroad station just as the others come back from the whorehouses. From then till now we have been loading wounded soldiers onto a hospital train. Stretcher after stretcher. Heartbreaking! The military hospitals and headquarters are being evacuated because the Tommy may be in Paris at any minute.
We run into soldiers from our division. They had managed to get through. The division is surrounded. Where are we going to end up? And how long will we be able to stay in this magnificent, enormous city?
What was I, a soldier or a tourist?

Charlons sur Marne, August 18, 1944
20:00. Last night shooting from windows near the Paris railway station. We were waiting for four buddies who finally got there at 22:30. Already by the Opera they had been shot at. There are wounded. Right in our midst a woman was shot through the chest.
She was lying on the pavement. Somebody knelt down, ripped her blouse

open. I had never seen my grown-up sister naked, nor my girlfriend. It was in Paris, city of love, where, for the first time, I saw a woman's breast. It gushed blood.

Left Paris this morning early. The Tommy is supposed to be in Versailles. Whatever is left of the German troops is leaving Paris. Retreat!

When will we be sent to the front? Nobody knows anything about the 9th Panzer Division which we are supposed to report to. Many are saying it makes no sense to go on fighting. Everyone should save his own life. Perhaps they're right?

We stayed in Nancy from August 20th to 26th waiting for things to develop. In Nancy we had to report in the Rommel-Barracks. Obviously, Rommel's involvement in the officers' revolt on July 20th 1944 was kept secret or the Barracks would have been re-named. I do remember that the name of another conspirator, Witzleben, had been painted over on one of the barracks that we passed through on our way west. I do not recall how I reacted to that assassination attempt. When it happened, I was on my last home leave, and apparently the big event did not evoke any echo in my journal nor my memory. All I remember is that afterwards the traditional army salute was forbidden and replaced by the Nazisalute; without "Heil Hitler," of course, but it looked and felt awkward enough especially if you carried something heavy and saw an officer coming…a situation for Schwejk or Chaplin…or you had to jerk your head to the side and keep it stiff till the superior had passed. The new salute would have been even more ridiculous had we known our future: the lucky ones among us were soon raising not one but both arms. In the POW camps the Nazi-salute was forbidden and the traditional military salute reestablished, that is for the POW-commander reporting to the British officer at roll call. The rest of us did not salute anybody; the German officers had their own camps, and we never saw them.

Drommeville, August 28, 1944
Finally we find the train of regiment nr. 10, the remains of the division. Of 100 transport carriers only four are left. Gently rolling hills. Lots of fruit around here. Gorge ourselves on green gages. Idyllic landscape.

Verdun, August 29, 1944
Yesterday the English took Chalons sur Marne. Now we are in Verdun. How dead the

country around here looks. Desolate. White clay soil gleams through dry grass. Traces of trenches of the Great War. The monumental memorial for the dead. 40,000 German soldiers. The buildings are of a blinding brightness, white like the clay in which they died. We were standing on the town square where we had a full view of the monument, and there we met Helmut Machata and Hansi Walter, two of our buddies from regiment 11. They had seen action. All the others were probably taken prisoner by the Tommy. Blass Hans was killed on a patrol—the first of our OCTU-group. Strange that we should get the news here in this town of death.

Our division was wiped out before we ever got to it, and our orders were to go east again to be reassigned in Germany. When we came to a strategic bridge, SS-men, pistol in hand, forced everybody back who wanted to cross without authorization. Our driver must have had that because we got to the other side. On German soil we went through the process of being "reassembled" just months before the Third Reich went to pieces.

Ebersweiler. September 1, 1944 — probably the date when my de facto front-line probation began.

Beginning of sixth year of war. In the west near Metz rumbling of artillery. Yankees. The Lothringians are evacuating the area. The Nazi-Party chief of Ebersweiler has been burning documents and pictures of Hitler in front of his house. In the smoking pile we find a book about Wehrmacht–reports of the campaign in France. Those were the days!

Lebach. September 2, 1944
On the drive during the night war was close. Slowly the rumbling behind us faded. The horizon flared up all in red-massive, beautifully red clouds; from time to time, they flared up more like sheet lightning announcing the coming thunderstorm of battle. We pass many horse-drawn carriages on which the peasants of the area want to take their belongings into safety. Here, too, the fighter-bomber wreaked havoc this afternoon: dead horses, overturned carts; back there, the two last horses lying in their blood on the road. Didn't we just hear them neighing? Cursed, damned fighter-bombers. Ammunition is exploding like fireworks. In Lebach we sleep in a hay barn till 10:00 this morning. In the afternoon, at the movies, and the title is "The Wild Night." It's striking that almost all the girls around here are pretty.

September 4, 1944
Lebach. Evening. Again beautiful weather today. We're lying in the sun, and alternate

between washing our shirts and socks. In the evening, alarm. We're supposed to go to Saarlautern to join a fighting unit to help in the eventual defence of Metz. It was a false alarm.

September 12, 1944
Near Aachen, we did see action after all. There are six men left of the 140. The rest are all dispersed. What a day that was! I won't forget the 9th of September very soon! Within a few hours the RAF fighter-bombers nearly wiped us out. We had to retreat through a forest. Direct hits of the artillery, etc. etc. I don't have to write all that down. My first exposure to heavy fire.

We were running like mad through the trees hoping that we would not be seen from the sky. But the fighter bombers were right over us and sprayed us with their 2cm bullets. A man running in front of me was hit in the back, the blood bubbled up in the gusts of the heart beat. A soldier had sunk down to the ground, leaning against a tree. One of his eyes was out, he was whimpering. "The medics will get you," somebody shouted as we pushed past him. Screams: "The Yanks are after us," "The Blacks!" That word evoked the rumoured atrocities of the Senegalese in World War I! We panicked. It was all terrifying and ridiculous. The Yanks were not anywhere near at that time. It was the RAF that was after us and kept firing, and we ran and ran. And then all of a sudden it was all over, we thought. A buddy and I got separated from the rest and found ourselves out of the wood in open farm country with hedges and ditches. Suddenly a low flying fighter bomber was chasing just the two of us like rabbits. We ran along hedges, played dead, ran on, cut sharp corners, but there they were again, curving low, coming back and always spitting bullets at us. It was almost as if they were out just to scare us and having a great time doing it. Years later I came across Kubin's pen and ink drawing of a man being pursued by huge flying insects and it brought back those tense moments. Thank God, there was a small brick farmhouse all by itself in the field and a woman came out and waved us in. We were safe, and the RAF-huntsmen were off after another prey. We went on trying to find our unit, and ended up in an air-raid shelter in an Aachen suburb. Our pants were torn and muddy, and there we were sitting down among the civilians. One upright citizen pleaded with the others to share some food for "our brave front-line soldiers." I wonder whether we looked as sheepish as we felt while we munched the sandwiches that were immediately handed us in true Volksgemeinschaft....

September 20, 1944
Last night we spent in an empty house. During the night the artillery hit again. In spite of that, it was very comfortable in the soft double beds with the red bedside lamp. The Front is now somewhat stabilized again. Here on German soil, the Americans won't get through so fast. Tonight we are going ahead to take our positions.

September 21, 1944
Last night we were pulled ahead to a hillside and were in enemy artillery fire immediately. We moved on to a house which had just been vacated; in the basement we slept, more or less. In the morning, we advance to the edge of the wood where we dig ourselves in. It's now 4:00 p.m; and I'm writing this sitting in my hole. There are still some engineers in front of us. The whole day the artillery is whizzing above us. Tsooee Tsooee Woomm. Their observer was circling overhead I took my rifle and shot at him, twice. He went on circling.

My two rifle shots were the only shots I fired in World War II. It is the only achievement I am proud of. I did not kill or wound anybody. I have no "heroic" stories to tell to my children and grandchildren and plant the "glory" of war in their minds.

September 24, 1944
Wild days are behind us. In the evening of the 21st, we, who had been in reserve up till then, were pulled forward to a bunker and then it was rifles against tanks. Wild artillery fire on the hedge where we had been before. In the dark all around the thud, thud of metal digging into the ground. It got our platoon leader, Nieschke, ripped off his leg, and he died on transport the same night. Then we are lying in a shallow dugout; above, the tracer bullets are whistling. Next to me, a dead German. A hole in his helmet. How peacefully he is lying there in his uniform—so new that I can see the plant fibre in the wartime material—and light brown leather belt and cartridge boxes, he's probably been there for some time by now. As I look at his waxy yellowish face and glassy eyes, I think of the mannequins in the Wehrmacht exhibition in Vienna. And there, in the shelled crater, in which I am lying, there is another one with a bashed-in head. Around the bunker, there are a few more men of our platoon. Many of them just beat it out of there. Amid enemy artillery strikes and German "friendly fire," somewhere out there, the wounded are calling. Night–things are getting quieter. We're sleeping in a basement in Donnerberg. This is really a thunder hill. Through the night, Americans in a truck or something are cruising around the place. Twenty yards away from us. We can hear them talk. But as soon as the long gun of a German Tiger tank appears round a corner down the block they take off in a hurry.

In the same lane, an ammunition truck is exploding in a first class fireworks display. Next morning, we retreat to Notberg. On the 23rd, I go up the hill with the Lieutenant once more. Everything is ok. They won't get through here! Some burnt-out Shermans are standing around. I see my first dead enemy lying outside a tank, all black and charred, burnt to half his size. Who is waiting for him back home? – They just won't make it here. Now the 12th Division is next to us and our artillery is working full-steam. In the early morning hours, we go back down to Bohl, where our passenger car is waiting, and drive to Notberg.

The passenger car was a requisitioned American model, a Buick or a Chevy, with benches in the back and on top of the cab, a machine gun mounted on a plywood board.

Our Division has been relieved. Today is Sunday, but someone would have to tell us that. The area around here is full of evacuees and the artillery is hitting the villages. War in Germany.

"Vee Vant To Surrender"

October 6, 1944

From a different situation I will try to recreate what had happened, to put the pieces together of what I remember of that chaotic day. Some of it I wrote in my journal (here in italics), other details I wrote down many years later. The day I was taken prisoner was October 1 1944, the date when the required month of my frontline probation de jure ended. I should have gone back to officers school to get my commission. The fact that I went somewhere else probably saved my life. I was lucky.

At 2 a.m. we started to move forward to assume our assembly position—in an open seemingly endless plain. Drizzle and fog slowly drifted over it. Only now and then shooting to the left and right of us; in our section it was quiet. At 6:00 am, after freezing in our dugouts for two hours we advanced through countless ditches, completely soaked we went from one to the next. It was still twilight and we could not see what was awaiting us ahead. Engineers were supposed to throw boards across the ditches for our advance but they never showed up. We were supposed to get tank support but the tanks never showed up either. Suddenly we got rifle fire from the right. I was the only O.C.T.U-cadet assigned to this particular unit and in charge of a dozen men, most of whom were old enough to be my father. When, duty-bound and stupid, I left cover to advance in imprudent moments, they shouted me back and saved my life. *We got to an orchard; fortunately the Tommy was shooting much too high. The branches of the fruit trees were crackling over our heads, explosive bullets were bursting.* I was watching a big soldier lying flat on the ground, legs spread far apart, and a young one crawling up to him from the back, desperate for cover, pressing his head against the big guy's buttocks. The big fellow was hit in the head and went limp. The young kid, realizing what had happened, panicked, got up screaming with terror and ran back. Was he lucky! I saw him again later. *Thanks to our machine gunner Nr. 1, we and the two lieutenants reached the farmhouse at the end of the garden.* We stormed in. I still remember seeing my first British Army jacket, not on a soldier but lying on the floor; somebody must have left in a hurry. *We left the house and went to the hay barn and rested.* Had we accomplished our mission? Not quite.

I can't recall the exact sequence of what happened. We went back and forth from barn to house to another barn while the Tommy was shooting at us. *The Tommy had let us get into the farm house and now we were in the trap. Where was the other company? Communication had completely broken down. The lineman for the artillery was with us but could not get through. Twice a messenger tried to get through the orchard. After a few jumps the Tommy shot at him. He was lucky to make it back to us.* At one point I was supposed to cover on the right, and, on the lieutenant's orders, told the machine gunner to set up his machine gun on the concrete floor of the barn with the barn gate wide open. He started firing against an invisible enemy. For not very long. He was too good a target. Bullets were hitting the concrete. Suddenly both his hands went to his head, and he raced back through the barn. I saw him later with a bandage round his head. *The Tommy machine gun was hacking away. It had registered the barn gate accurately, and the bullets went through the barn, a connecting corridor, and straight through the kitchen. We told the civilians to wave white rags and beat it*—to safety, presumably. Suddenly a tank appeared out of the mist. Our support at last! No such luck. It was a British model, and began firing tank grenades at us. When the barn went up in flames, we stormed back into the house. When the house caught fire we ran down into the cellar. Some of us had left our rifles upstairs and were not going to retrieve them out of the blaze. When the flames reached the top cellar stairs we rushed up through them and out. One officer offered an Iron Cross First Class to anyone who would sneak up to the tank and finish it with a panzerfaust. The demand for Iron Crosses, First or any other class, had reached a low point. Nobody moved. The officer didn't either; he had the Iron Cross already. And the Tommy kept shooting; a second tank appeared. *The situation was hopeless.*

Afterwards, we talked about our feelings while the bullets were whizzing overhead and the tank shells were bursting in the air and on the roof and haybarn and all. One of my best chums, an Austrian from Linz said "You know, I really saw Jesus and he told me not to worry." I myself thought of absolutely nothing. I was not afraid. I was not hopeful. I simply was lying there. I didn't think "so that's it.' No, I was conscious, very conscious, but I didn't think. It was an exemplary existentialist situation.

There were two civilian earth bunkers, or were they root cellars? A bunch of soldiers rushed in. I couldn't get in anymore and I tried to dig myself in by deepening the entrance to the cellar. That didn't seem safe enough. I threw myself into a smoking shell crater. Just in time. The bunker got a direct hit. Some men tried to get back out through the orchard. The tank guns got them and the grenade throwers, and they were torn to bits. The situation was hopeless. *The men wanted to surrender. One took a white rag and ran out. The Tommy's machine gun was hacking at him. He came right back.* One of the officers thought we should surrender as a group. *Give the order!* The men shouted. *The lieutenant did: "Surrender!"*

We emptied our cartridge boxes, threw the weapons we still had on a heap. And that's where my neat little Spanish pistol ended up, too. Our group slowly walked down the gently sloping meadow; the lieutenant, supporting a lightly wounded soldier on either arm, was limping. They looked like a poster for the war effort. We kept walking. To make the obvious blatant, I snatched a dishtowel from the household mess that was strewn around, a white one with red stripes, thin red stripes, so that most of the cloth was white, waved it like mad and shouted in my high school English, "Vee vant to surrrender." Where, in the high school of the Third Reich, had I ever picked up such a treacherous word? But there it was, and my dishtowel action, combined with my questionable linguistic skill, was my only real action in World War II. And I felt quite brave. My screaming was answered with dead silence on the other side. They were not dead, of course, but they did not shoot. God bless the Geneva Convention! Suddenly there were Tommies all over; they just jumped up from nowhere, that is from the ditches, and they were tall. Irish Guards, as we found out. One of these giants reached out to help me out of the ditch and, as he was pulling me up, I saw that his forearm up to his elbow, was ringed with wrist watches–good thing I had hidden my grandfather's silver watch in my boot. And all the time he was shouting over our heads "Maak snell" in that Anglo-Saxon German that I was to hear so often teaching my mother tongue in Montana; in every beginning class, whenever we came across the word "schnell," I recalled that moment in 1944. His German was about as bad as my English. *The front line reception wasn't bad at all. Then a bit later we were lined up facing a brick wall, hands over our heads. A machine gun was stationed behind us pointing at our backs, and we feared the worst. Then there was a click, and the Tommies laughed, and the dreadful spell was broken.*

And then something interesting happened. After the first line of Tommies, there was a second. And this time, they were not such intimidating giants; they looked pretty ordinary, slightly underfed working class chaps. A small guy, shorter than I, suddenly stood in front of me and frisked me to be sure I wasn't a fanatic carrying arms behind British lines. And as this enemy came so close to me, I was afraid and trembled, and I saw him quite close up and, as he was fumbling down my arms and legs, he was trembling, too. And I could see that he had never done this before, that I probably was his first enemy close up, and he was afraid. What a farce such a war is. I have never forgotten my comrade in fear. And he didn't even do a good job. Later, when we were behind rows of barbed wire, I discovered he had overlooked the egg hand grenade in my back pants pocket. I took the charge out and buried it at night, so that the guards wouldn't see me doing it.

There is another impression of that day, as vivid today as it was fifty years ago. Since I spoke some kind of English, I was interrogated by a British officer who, gentleman that he was, gave me a metal cup of good, bracing English tea with milk and sugar. The tea smelled good; for years we had only drunk kinds of tea that foreshadowed the herbal bliss of today's Health Food Stores. But it was a different smell that impressed me much more: the smell of real, genuine gasoline. It was all over between the trucks and the tanks, and the smell told me, once and for all, that Germany had lost the war. But did that message really sink in at the time? The journal is more honest. In it I followed what all the other good soldiers around me believed, even behind barbed wire, that the German fight against her powerful enemies was far from lost. And all the news to the contrary that we were constantly hearing in the camps was but enemy propaganda not to be believed.

On trucks we were transported away from the Front. Everywhere troops, trucks, tanks! How different it had looked from the German side. On an open field surrounded by barbed wire they frisked us again and took watches and all sorts of other things from us. In the last minute I let grandfather's pocket watch glide down in my crotch assuming correctly that they wouldn't touch me there, and my journal, too, I saved. In the middle of the night on to another open compound. Soldiers were sleeping in holes they had dug in the wet gravel.

There wasn't much food. Next day there was a chance to get more–if you were willing to bury the dead Americans that had come down in pieces in those gliders near Arnheim. But the volunteers–and I was not one of them–were so sick after what they had seen and had to do that they could not enjoy their reward. One of the burying crew got something out of it: proudly he showed us a brand new pair of American parachuter boots, but he could not eat a bite of the German can of goulash he was awarded.

Pow Camps
Belgium
Enghien

October 1, 1944.   *32 km west of Brussels.*
We are in a former nunnery, can finally wash and, for the first time in five days: warm coffee plus German Africa Corps biscuits and this morning one tablespoon of jam. Right now we are debating the general situation. Maybe we should have waited for the night on that Oct 1 and fought our way back? Perhaps?? At any rate, we are alive. And so far the treatment by the Tommies has not been humiliating. That had been only the case with the Military Police. –If we only were in a stable camp and could write home. If only mother would get news from me before getting the missed-in-action notice from the company.

There were several interrogations. One of them I remember especially well, this time by Canadian officers. They asked me "Why do you think we came all the way from Canada to fight this war?," and I said "I think you're just adventurers." When the officer told his buddies what I had said, they roared with laughter. And then I said I would like to be sent to a camp in Canada because "I want to see the world at your expense." And they laughed again, and the officer said "Will Great Britain do?"

October 4, 1944
Since yesterday five others from our company and I are part of the base personnel of this POW Transit camp. The chaos is boundless since right now there are 3,500 prisoners here. Being the base personnel we are supposed to get additional rations. But the Tommy puts that off day after day. Today 1,000 are to leave the camp. As far as I am concerned, I'd love to be one of them if I only knew where they are going. To England I'd go at once.

October 7, 1944
Twice a day we get biscuits, once a day a jar of jam for 16 men, and a two pound can of stew for four. Today I made myself a canteen (autumn model 1944): a tin can with a

handle.

October 10, 1944
I hope we will soon be sub-divided into smaller camps because here conditions are awful. There are more than 1,000 men here, and the food situation is terrible. We are always hungry. However, today we got tea twice, and perhaps tomorrow we can count on a warm lunch. Good thing that one of us is in the kitchen.

October 16, 1944
Whenever the food comes someone else is dividing it up, and everybody presses forward to get as close to him as possible to watch and be sure that he is not being disadvantaged. Every milligram of food counts. Our cleaning group of the base personnel is better off. We were even supposed to have warm food, warm food for the first time in 16 days. And it was true, we did get soup, carrot soup, but not enough of it. Our group, that is the six of us, got a quarter of a loaf of white bread (but what white bread!). And some liver sausage spread. The others are looking in at the door. First they mocked us as the dirt gang, now they would have liked to storm our "cell." Our group is working out alright. There must be some order. After a while hunger would turn all of us into animals. But things are getting better, that must be due to the new English Camp Commander Sergeant who speaks for us.

October 18, 1944
Got so much food that we live almost better than in the German Army. Still, we would rather do without the grub, if we could be back again. Especially today our thoughts go back home. We all got a card to write home. Will it ever get there?

October 19, 1944
Today two POWs got into a fight because one of them spat on the floor. The filth and the unsanitary behaviour is beyond description. They're pissing into the canister that the tea comes in. Some are exchanging their war medals for cigarettes. Did they ever deserve getting a medal? How self-righteous! How did I know how fed up with the war and everything they might have been? I had never smoked; and couldn't understand why some men would even fish the tea dregs out of the canisters and dry them for tobacco.
What is going on at the front? We have no idea. The Tommy says that he is in Cologne. At the same time we hear that German tanks are threatening Brussels. – Again and again there are fights with Polish POWs. This damn fighting!

October 22, 1944
Sunday today. The third behind barbed wire. Today another transport left for Ostend, as

they say. I would have liked to go with them. But even for us, who are hungry for experience, the time will come. Every night, some POWs disappear, but again and again, they're hauled back. The Tommies are watching like hawks. I'm trying to get as many English newspapers as I can. I'm always glad to get a new one. Wild rumours are going around. Hungary has capitulated. The Russians have penetrated Slovakia and stand in front of Brno. Of course I don't believe it, but my thoughts cannot avoid the possibility that the Front gets closer to Vienna.

October 29, 1944
Neglected my journal in the last few days since we are always reading English newspapers or books. Now I'm reading The Grey Ghost, *a fantastic science fiction novel from the last century. It's always so nice to discover what it's all about. Just now a soldier was here who wanted to exchange his golden wedding ring for four cigarettes. In the room across from ours, Franz's band is playing. Our Swabian Karl is drumming on an empty box, Franz is playing the mandolin, and two spoons add to the music. Some tunes sound quite acceptable, but if you hear them all the time...*

November 1, 1944
Don't feel well, chills; Rudi has a temperature. Foggy weather, a real All Souls Day. The only bright spot: the hope to get to England.

JABEKKE

November 3, 1944
On the first we left after all. We passed a Belgian town with the "friendly" population who greeted us enthusiastically, that is they gave the victory sign to our English guards, to us gestures of "Heads-off." We spent the night in a camp of tents, but in our German overcoats we were warm. The next morning the sun was shining and some of us strolled around in the camp and overheard the command for rollcall. Suddenly, I heard behind me, "And you, are we supposed to send an extra telegram?" and an Officer hits us on the back with his swagger cane. I got a blow on the back of my head so that I had a bump for several days. So that's what those little sticks are for. The rollcall was taken right on the road and many Belgian girls drove by, looking at our faces as if looking for somebody in particular.

November 8, 1944
We have been here now for a week and we are together with the railroad POWs. Five of us sleep on the concrete floor. There are two more bunks above us; it's quite drafty down here. Yesterday, suddenly, we heard English flak and stormed out, glad that the Luftwaffe was still around. Many soldiers escape from this camp. At one time, twenty of them stole

an English machine gun and took off with it. (Later we heard that in some camps American black soldiers even helped German POWs, or just looked the other way.) *Actually, I feel less of a pull to go back east, but rather on to England or Canada, where I can experience something of the wide world. Now they have reinforced the barbed wire to make it more difficult to get away.*

November 11 1944.
Tonight there was a birthday party for one of us. A small group sang folksongs. Someone had written a poem about being a POW, and our Communist, who had a beautiful bass voice, made up a tune for it. It was all rather emotional and, at one point, he could not go on any more, he was crying... By now the Missing in Action Notices must have been mailed. When I think of that and Mother...
I was right.

    Office of Fieldpost Nr.19884   31.10.1944

    Dear Mrs. Jarka

    Since the heavy defensive operations near Elst, 8 km southwest of Arnheim on October 1, 1944 your son, O.T.C.U. Corporal Horst Jarka, has not returned to his unit. Our efforts to find him were of no avail, and since then we have had no indication of his whereabouts. The circumstances prevailing at that time make it possible that he was taken prisoner. I have not written earlier because I always hoped that your son would return to his unit. I may assure you that your son always was a good and exemplary fellow soldier and I share your wish that he may return in good health after the final victory.

           In sincere sympathy and with Heil Hitler!
                        Yours
                      [Signature]
           Lieutenant and Company Commander

Mother did not give up. The letter from the commander of the battalion was the same as that of the Company commander, only the Major signed without Heil Hitler.

November 13, 1944
In an English paper I read about the V2, a fantastic weapon which flies through the air

This was the poem sung at the birthday party on November 11

The Wedding Ring that Went Up in Smoke

Far in Belgium by the sea,
Behind barbed wire, cold and damp,
Captured German soldiers stand
Freezing in the British camp.

Sadly they walk up and down,
Through the wire sea winds sting.
They are all worn out and hungry.
No one now can laugh or sing.

But a forty year old soldier
Has but one thought in his head:
"If I only had a smoke now,
Tobacco I need more than bread."

Twisting off his wedding ring
He reaches through the wire fence
And offers it, in his despair,
To the sentry posted there.

"Give me cigarettes he pleads.
The sentry grins and grabs the ring.
Gives him three whole fags in pay.
And nmerrily he goes his way.

German Fräuleins, German Fraus,
German menfolk you can trust,
But oh great God in your high heaven
For cigarettes they'll break their vows.

Dedicated to the street singer Bartokos
For his heartfelt rendition.
From a fellow POW in camp Jabekke,
November 8th, 1944

and carries 40 tons of explosives.

The "miracle weapon" as it was called. It would ensure German victory in the end. The miracle was that we actually believed that.

November 17, 1944
Today we got stamped like cattle. SECRET, that's what we have on our forearm, so that tomorrow no one will get on the boat who is not on the list.

And so I was shipped to Great Britain from Ostende in a troop tanker. The trip took hours and hours because they had to zigzag between the mines in the Channel, and when we finally landed at the Tilbury Dock in the Thames Estuary, we were lifted up to the deck in the open elevator and the wind took my cap away, and on the shore there were WAAFS singing "Lili Marleen" for welcome, and offering us hot tea. Jolly old England!

Then soldiers took over and impatiently waved us on and rushed us onto lorries or was it a train? I don't remember; I do remember what they shouted: "Come on, get a move on, gentlemen!," not in English but in a very familiar dialect "Gemma, gemma, meine Herr'n!" Refugees from Vienna.

England

November 20, 1944
Kempton Park Race Course.
Last night, we had to eat on the double and then a night in a tent. But it was cosy, since there were enough blankets. This morning again first class white bread and cake. Then a warm bath. Our clothes were disinfected and our valuables were taken away. (Journal and Faust) Then we were interrogated I had a conversation with a Tommy officer, quite interesting, about the general situation. I asked him about the V-I and V-II, and why Americans were fighting in Europe. He said that Hitler claimed world power, and the USA was threatened from the south because of the big German influence in South America. Now we are finally clean and not hungry.

We got on a passenger train with upholstered plush seats. I had never been in an elegant train like this. At home we rode on wooden benches and in the army in freight cars for "12 horses or 40 men." We moved slowly through the outskirts of London, past bombed houses with tarps instead of roofs. We did not hear what the people in the houses and in the streets were shouting at us. They were shaking their fists at us and throwing stones which amused us because they were throwing them against their own railroad cars, and occasionally, one would hit but no windows were broken.

Via Canonberry we came to Sheffield on Nov. 29 in the early morning. In double decker buses we drove through the city in dense fog. The dark outlines of the unlit street lamps made the fog even spookier. Sherlock Holmes. Our destination:

Camp 17, Sheffield

The camp command was Polish. We were newly registered, and I was given a new number B 30239, a white kitbag, and a set of new underwear. I did not write much in my journal during the weeks before Christmas. Memory is more reliable apart from the dates. One event I did not record but recall very clearly, and it probably happened during those first weeks in Sheffield. Air raid alarm! It was night. Excited, we rushed out in our long underwear. The searchlights at the corners of the camp that usually lit up the length of the fences were turned straight up into the sky (as required by the Geneva Convention), but there was no droning of planes overhead. In our area we heard a soft rhythmic purr: the V-1 going over us in the direction of Manchester. The Tommy guards were flat on their bellies and we were laughing at them and cheering the rocket: "Hinein!" "Hinein!" something like "Give it to them!" We forgot that these rockets were not at all accurate, and we might have been wiser to be on the ground with the Tommies.

December 24, 1944
Christmas in a POW camp. There is something romantic about this. I miss the green branches and the snow. We get 40 cigarettes, 2 pieces of cake and toothpaste! In the evening we light our sailor's tree (made of bare sticks). "Silent night, holy night." In the moonlight I stroll from wire to wire. The stars are sparkling. We pass the rest of the evening with chess and mock tests of our school learning.

December 29, 1944
Cheerful New Year's Party. Handshaking all around. "Happy New Year!" A parade round the barracks. And we sing: "Denn wir fahren gegen Engelland. – "We're on our way to England!" – the song that had been blaring over the German radio and the loudspeakers in every classroom when the U-boats had scored a hit again. Were any of us aware that we had no need to be "on our way" since we already were in "Engelland"? I wish I could say that I saw the irony of it all, but I doubt it; more likely, I sang with the others just as loudly as I had

cheered the V1 on its mission of death and destruction.
January 13, 1945
Last night a cabaret evening by some Viennese. Quite nice, Viennese songs including:
>*And who will now sweep our streets?*
>*And who will now sweep out streets?*
>*The officer gents*
>*With red stripes down their pants*
>*They're the ones to sweep our streets. Hallo!*

Mother had often told me how in 1918 *soldiers coming back from the front had sung that song in Vienna. How strange it was to hear it in a POW camp in England! When the pianist started playing the best-known march of the Austro-Hungarian army "We are the infant-er-ry Regiment Number four" there were shouts from the back of the room: "Stop it! Stop! Be glad the war's over. D'ya want another one!?"*
Some of our compound cut the fence and crawled over to the neighbouring one. They all came back just in time, except for one guy from the navy. Will that be a ruckus again!

January 22, 1945
The "Quartermaster" betrayed the Paratrooper Sergeant and, together with the Czech camp guards, beat him up for a whole hour. Gagged. Nose broken, his arm broken in two places.

I did not record the details and I don't remember any. The Austrians were afraid the Germans would get reinforcements from the other compound (through the hole) in the fence and beat up the Austrians. A feud developed between Austrians and Germans. In the night the Tommy came, counted our heads, and confiscated all stoking irons and coal shovels.

I hope we manage to get out of this international camp.

I didn't want to have anything to do with such senseless fights and conflicts.

January 23, 1945
A big disappointment with a buddy from whom I would never have expected it. I had lent him my Faust *and he forgot it somewhere, and now it's gone. I'll remember that!*

In another camp someone had stolen my cap, and now my Faust *was "lost." What next? The Tommies came back for another search. They were after a swastika flag. Now we are in a tent camp. Nine men in a tent. There is a good little stove in ours and we are sitting around it. There is no end to the discussion; no wonder, our socialist (or communist?), the chess champion, is amongst us.*

He said he had been in a Concentration Camp, but would not talk about it. I wish I could remember some of the discussion. What I do remember is hardly intellectual; the nine of us had to sleep close together under too many, too heavy blankets. And they were not very clean. We found lots of lice in the seams of our long underwear and spent hours cracking them between our fingernails like real front line soldiers—in Sheffield!

January 27, 1945
Last night one of the tents was burning. The screaming! All got out but they lost all their meagre belongings. Now we always keep a knife ready so that we can slit the tent open if necessary.

February 2, 1945
Took up whittling again. Made a chess set of hard wood.

February 8, 1945
Evening with Arthur Schneider. Read Faust *together and talked about it, and then sang songs. A fellow in our hut has built himself a real violin, and he plays it every evening. The violin is weeping with a longing that we have not felt for a long time.*

February 13, 1945
At last the courses have started. Teachers are excellent. We speak about Faust.

February 16, 1945
Radio reports, Vienna bombed. Are we ever going to see our home again?

February 17, 1945
Lecture about forestry, highly interesting to me.

February 22, 1945
Spent the evening with poems and passages from Faust. *We also have a choir now; I went there as listener, rather folksy.*

February 26 1945
Lecture about the Age of Rembrandt. "His works may be destroyed at this very moment, but his legacy in our hearts and this our German striving cannot be imprisoned by barbed wire and not extinguished by bombs."

And I must have been impressed with this verbiage or I would not have written down every word.
When I left the lecture barrack the moon looked through the cloudy sky in the west and in the dark eastern sky a rainbow spanned its arc in subdued colours. Did not Rembrandt's art try to approach the colours of nature from yellow orange to violet? Or did he create a mystic darkness so that the light would radiate all the brighter? I have seen a rainbow

at night! — the only interesting and memorable event that evening. *Cases of homosexuality.*

They held one of the boys and shaved his head while he, in desperate defiance, was shouting again and again: "I can do with my body what I want."

February 27, 1944
Just back from a variety show. Individual scenes were played wonderfully. In spite of the modest means the sets were very good, and I liked the whole thing very much. The women's roles were absolutely realistic in their disguises.

March 3, 1944
Red Cross shipment: black bread, three pieces of candy, a small piece of ginger bread, and four plums. They should pass these things out at home not here.

March 7, 1944
I'm in the sick ward with a nasty rash; started to write my autobiography—at the ripe age of nineteen and a half. I did not get beyond the age of six or seven.

March 8, 1944
In bed, both legs smeared with sulphur ointment. I am sorry to miss the lectures.

March 11, 1945
Both legs up to my arse in white bandages. That eczema doesn't want to heal. I am so sorry to miss the lectures.

March 12, 1945
Many of the teachers have been transferred to other camps. That's the end of the courses.

March 14, 1945
Last night we heard some shots from a machine pistol. This morning we found that POWs in compound 2 had thrown stones at the English sentry, and he had fired. The result of all this stupidity was that a completely innocent young fellow taking his evening jog in gym shorts came round the kitchen corner and was killed. Now everybody blames the English soldier. But a German soldier would not have acted differently.

March 15, 1945
Among the the new arrivals there's a Viennese who was at home at Christmas. He said that the West Railroad Station had been damaged, and that the trams weren't running anymore.

March 16, 1945
I wrote home, but have almost given up hope of ever getting any mail from back there.

March 25, 1945

Big raid by the Tommies yesterday. Searches. A long tunnel had been discovered, from the hut where the church services were held underground to the fence. They had hidden the dirt under the benches in the church. *Everything was betrayed The traitors were beaten up, and one of them died* an hour later.

March 28, 1945

I'm back in our hut and sleep in my own bed. Too bad that there are so many new faces around. I have just seen some theatre, quite nice: scenes from Faust. Auerbach's Tavern, *farcical scenes by Hans Sachs; the* Wanderer from Paradise, Till Eulenspiegel *and* The Blind. *Outside the full moon! The spring wind races from the west and tugs at my feelings. The more spring is in the air, the deeper the barbed wire cuts into me. Now I really feel what freedom is. The Tommy writes in his papers that his army is in front of Nurnberg. To believe it is madness, But it is enough that they are on the other side of the Rhine. How is it all going to end? I am taking part in the courses again, but I don't know, sometimes I feel like cursing all this baggage of knowledge. That's my mood today. Perhaps only because I missed so much of the courses, and I can't discipline myself to catch up. But I'll have to do it, certainly in maths and German. But, instead of going to classes, I prefer walking around now that the weather is so mild. I met my 56-year-old friend from the sick ward. He is in the other compound, and we have to talk through the wire.*

Today I even managed to scrounge up a nib. Such an insignificant thing otherwise, but now how important! The nib and the ink that I brewed myself are my only writing utensils.

March 31, 1945

Now I often walk over to the hut of the teacher to copy poems by Goethe, Mörike, Hölderlin. There's going to be a lecture to give us at least some special feelings about the Easter holiday. I found a poem a few days ago, and was happy with the find. Schiller's "Die Hoffnung"–"Hope," a typical calendar poem for school textbooks, but for me it did what it was supposed to do: 'give me strength' ...and my next letter to mother I started with a quote from the poem and its moral:

> How grateful we are for a few precious words. Is it not hope that we all build upon? The hope that everything will turn out well, the hope to see each other again? Are we not all at the mercy of relentless fate? Hope is the only thing left. The news of the last few days make me think often of you and worry about you. It is a dreary Easter this year. Easter? If the calendar didn't tell us, we wouldn't know. Dismal rain whipped by the storm against our hut, the sky hidden by dark clouds like the future. But are we to despair because

of that? The sun will shine again; the Mozart lecture we will hear tonight will be our sun.

Necessary as it was to occupy our minds with something, the offerings in literature were limited to the classics in a traditional way. In none of the camps that I was in was there any talk about modern, let alone foreign writers. The lectures and courses were, not by design but by the circumstances, exercises in maintaining our national identity through the strength of tradition. No attempt was made to reflect or to put our situation into a wider, critical perspective. There was a POW newspaper in German that included articles about English life, but I don't remember ever any discussion about them. And the camp command undertook no instruction about German politics past or present, because the Geneva Convention prohibited anything that might be interpreted as "political indoctrination." I, like the other prisoners, thought about home, and the culture that was offered was part of that home...as it had once been. The "theatre" that we saw consisted of comic scenes for entertainment; there were no actors to offer more. The constant changes from camp to camp did not allow the formation of any consistent troupe. But even among the funny skits there were no satires about camp life. Humour about our everyday situation would have been one way to overcome our self-involvement. In my journal there is no indication that I felt any need of different cultural offerings. There might have been some different courses offered, but I did not know of them or did not attend them. I seemed to be perfectly content with the general cultural, and my own personal, solipsism. Among my clippings from the German language POW newspaper, I find small print quotes from Goethe to remind us of the humanistic values of German classicism:

Edel sei der Mensch,	Man be noble
Hilfreich und gut	Helpful and good
Denn das allein	For that alone
Unterscheidet ihn	Distinguishes him
Von allen Wesen,	From all other creatures
Die wir kennen…	That we know…

but also two from Karl Kraus' *The Last Days of Mankind*:
>
> The dogs of war.
> We're pulling evil goods and yet we pull
> For we are loyal to the hour of death.

Camp 17- Sketch by H. Jarka, "I didn't even know how to spell the word I heard most often: 'Focking!'"

> How beautiful it was when God's sun was shining—
> The devil called, and the dogs followed.

And lines indicting man for what war has done to Creation:

> Through human might, through human deed
> I have turned grey. Once I was green.
> Look at me now.
> I was a wood, I was a wood,
>
> In my cathedral, you Christians hear!
> The soul found its eternal Rome.
> And in my silence was the Word
> Your actions were murder.
>
> Cursed be you who have done this to me.
> Never again will I rise up to heaven
> How green I was, now I am old
> I was a wood. I was a wood.

These verses Mother had often recited from memory. Did I see the tragic ironic contrast between the quotes from Goethe and those from Kraus? I did not comment on them in the journal. Did I cut out verses by Kraus only because they reminded me of Mother? Was Kraus ever mentioned in any of the lectures? I would have noted that, but then I missed many of them.

April 2, 1945
This morning we are transported from Camp 17 to Sheffield Station, by train to Manchester. There we march through the city in our "lovely" get-up to another station.

Camp 189 Dunham Park, Altrincham

April 7, 1945
The spring sun is warm and the many trees and bushes are budding. Only the oaks stretch their bare branches into the cloudless blue sky. This camp is much larger than the camp in Sheffield, and you can really stretch your legs. The kitchen is on the other side of the camp, the lines are long, and roll call takes a long time. But the food is tastier here than in Sheffield. There is a theatre here and today even a mobile movie theatre arrived. That's how well we live here while the Russians are advancing into Austria. They have pushed

west south of Vienna encircling the city. Today it was on the news that Klosterneuburg, my home town, has fallen. Shall I ever see Mother and Ruth and Ilse again? And in what state shall we find our home country, Vienna, the Kahlenberg, the places of childhood? I have no mind to read or do anything, and walk around under the tall trees that could be out of a fairy tale book.

April 9, 1945
Today I could have gone to a work camp but I preferred the known to the uncertain and stayed here.
Talking about the good food in this camp:

Every morning we used to have oats cooked in milk and apricot halves in it. When there were no apricots for a few days, an investigation discovered that the Austrian cook had made himself and his cronies apricot dumplings, Viennese style. The big debate about what to do with him resulted in the wise decision that, as long as apricots appeared in our hot cereal again, he should be retained. He had already stuffed himself, and a new cook would only just start fattening himself. The apricots returned, but now somebody complained of soot flakes in the oats. He was so worried that he even went to the camp doctor who consoled him: "Soot has never hurt anybody."

April 15, 1945
This morning the huts were decorated with numerous hammer-and-sickle-emblems in whitewash. And last night an Austrian flag waved from one of the treetops. The hammers and sickles disappeared, the flag stayed.

"Vienna liberated!" the English papers say. And we live here so peacefully and let the sun shine on us. Are Mother and Ruth still alive? Is there any sense in going back there?

These were the days when Dresden was bombed, but I don't remember that anybody even talked about it. Vienna was more important to me and the other Austrians in the camp.

April 17, 1945
This morning I've had to pull grass along the road that passes the camp. For a short time we were even on the sidewalk outside of the barbed wire. But the Poles of the Polish Legion were walking behind us. We didn't have to work much, so we watched the busy traffic. Brand new cars were driving behind beat up rattletraps. We even saw some pretty young English women, but they all had such pale faces. And then some caravans came, painted in gay colours and pulled by heavy draft horses. Inside, I could see bright clothes and even furnishings with mirrors and a tiny stove. In front, people with black hair, dark skin and

white flashing teeth, which seemed to be the only clean thing on them. Gypsies! They laughed and waved to us.

April 26, 1945
Keep busy with Uhland, astronomy, and English. Our hut is close to the road and almost constantly I hear cars and trucks go by. One sounds just like the buses at home that I could hear before falling asleep.

May 1, 1945
A few days ago an Austrian government was formed: Dr. Renner, Social Democrat, is the head of State. The First of May Celebration today is also a celebration of the Liberation of Austria.

May 4, 1945
After one month in Camp 189, on May 2nd we were shipped to a place near Bristol.

WALES
CAMP 197, CHEPSTOW

The camp was on a race course. There were bleachers and in front of them roll call was taken–one day in a grotesque spectacle. While the commanding officer accepted the report that so and so many hundreds of POWs were assembled before him in due order, a huge swastika flag was let down from the top of the grandstand behind him. Or had it been there before he came?

If he knew that it was there or not, nothing seemed to faze him while he did his duty. After all, what did these Nazi Krauts try to prove with their high school prank, now that the war was over? Where had the flag come from? The story was that the "rebels" had coloured a bed sheet with the dust of bricks; the rest had been easy. The flag was taken down and as far as I remember nothing happened if they ever found out who had done it at all. Nobody seemed to care really, the English least of all. Another incident in that camp stuck in my memory: In the compound next to ours some POW had caught a rather large bird, the size of a small crow perhaps. He had built a cage around it, and he was very proud of his catch and the cage. The other soldiers stood around him, teasing the bird with a stick. Prisoners caged in by barbed wire getting a kick out of teasing a caged creature!

May 8, 1945

This morning we heard the English victory bells! Since three p.m. there is supposed to be an armistice at the Western Front! Hitler dead! Germany destroyed!

May 11, 1945

We are experiencing the first days of peace. In Germany supposedly a catastrophic chaos is reigning. Nothing to eat. No water supply in the cities. But I'm not worried too much about Mother and Ruth in this respect because there are enough springs in our area. What I worry about is where they are. At home? Are they still alive?

One day we were shown a film about the Concentration Camps, the piles of skeletons, corpses. I could not believe it. German soldiers don't do that sort of thing! I don't know what others thought or said. There was no discussion that I remember. I only remember the shock and the disbelief, and that for a couple of days we got only water and little to eat. The horror did not sink in. I was worried about Mother and Ruth, and my fears blocked out everything else.

Today another shipment of packages came, including some private packages. I watched the unloading and noticed one that was covered by a white material and the address was written in indelible pencil. That's how the packages from Mother used to look! Since the German capitulation I think we are no longer bound by any oath and therefore, since May 7, 1945, I am an Austrian by nationality. The other buddies are of the same opinion.

May 20, 1945

Whitsun. It's pouring, as it was at Easter. Only that painfully I'm thinking of Whitsun last year–I was still at home for three days! At home!

June 3, 1945

I've found a pal who has studied forestry for two semesters; he's sitting beside me now and writing. His name is Theo. Theo is conducting a class in the form of a workshop. It's been raining now for several days. What a summer! Well, our climate does depend on water. From the bleachers of the race course building, we can see the water on two sides: that's the Bristol Channel–(today we had cocoa pudding for dessert! How long is it since I have eaten something like that!!)

June 14, 1945

I don't get along with Theo too well all the time, and the reason is that he is, for me, too much of a bourgeois, but I have found Gerhard Wuster, with whom I take many strolls around the camp and can talk about any topic. He is thirty-six years old, but young at heart. Our thoughts in close union drift out into space. How wonderful it is not to stand alone in this loneliness among hundreds of people. From him I also get English reading material which I am trying to plod my way through. For some days now, I have been taking a course in Russian.

It did not last long. The camp commander stopped it. The English did not want us to learn Russian. The Cold War had started before the hot one was hardly over... at least in Europe.

June 18, 1945

What a marvellous Sunday it was yesterday. Finally the sun that we had been waiting for so long was laughing. In the early morning I was right back in the corner, the quietest place in the camp where the two ash trees, the two maples, and the elm tree stand, and where the high beech trees beckon across the barbed wire.

I jotted down some verses praising the early morning, the sun: the blades of grass turning to the sun, the drew drops glistening, the clear air and everything that would chase away my gloom.

The same morning there was a kind of constitutional for one hundred and fifty men marching in quick step—and singing! But it was still very nice. As I was looking at the small houses with the blossoming roses in front of them, I threw a glance into a window, and saw there the cosy parlour in its dark coolness, and I imagined being in a different world There, at the little house at the beginning of the avenue of poplars, couldn't that be Eichendorff's Taugenichts *(The Good-for-nothing!) sitting in his red morning gown with yellow dots, and blowing the blue smoke out of his long-stemmed meerschaum up to the roof, entwined by lovely dark, red roses—? But also a melancholy feeling crept over me as I was feeling the Sunday peace of flowers and trees and human beings, as I saw the children standing in the flowers, looking at us wide-eyed. How many children will be standing now in Germany like that, waiting—waiting for those who were marching beside me—yes, at home, too, the flowers will be blooming, but the peace is missing—as in our hearts.*

June 22, 1945

Gerhard has given me a royal present. He has given me a nib because, since he is a medical orderly, he gets paid! The day before yesterday, I put my name down when the word spread that they're training elementary school teachers! That too would be a way into the future... It has been nice for several days now, the sun has been so warm and all day we have been lying in front of the huts sunning ourselves. As I was looking at the waving blades of grass beside me and looked up into the glorious blue sky, and as the snow white clouds were carrying my thoughts with them, I saw myself again at home in the garden under the walnut trees where now the red current bushes soon will bear fruit, or sitting up in the fork of a cherry tree surrounded by the wonderful red glory—how come I was thinking of fruit? Well, the rations have become meagre again. According to the Daily Express *in Styria, all men between sixteen and sixty, and women between sixteen and fifty, must work under supervision. If I imagine that happening at home, thank God Mother is over fifty, but one doesn't have to believe everything that the free press is reporting.*

June 26, 1945
I just came back again from an interrogation. Perhaps it could be possible to be transferred to a camp for Austrians, but what is also important: to be trained as an elementary school teacher while I am still a POW, a profession I would enjoy.

July 1, 1945
Now I've been behind barbed wire for nine months. Sunday! In spite of the meagre rations, I did take part again in our Sunday march. We went the same way as two weeks ago, and from the hill we could see the Bristol Channel, and beyond it factory smoke stacks of a city in the fog. We passed a gigantic linden tree, in full bloom. The wind carried the sweet scent to me—At home too the linden are blooming. Where are you now? Three years ago I saw you for the first time, and ever since I have seen only you, your hair waving in the wind, your laughing eyes, heard your voice beside me even when you were far away. There were painful hours; in spite of everything my longing goes out to you, as it goes out to my home country. I was so sure of that today as the breeze from the linden made me melancholy. —Ilse!

July 4, 1945
Last night it was so awfully warm that I couldn't fall asleep. Suddenly, word after word came to me:

    A poem about love and the linden tree. Ilse never saw it.

This morning, as I was standing in the damp drizzle, it spoke to me: "grey, heavy, the sky is pressing down." Another poem—this time about fog and rain, and dreariness in the camp and beyond the barbed wire in this country—and back home.

July 8, 1945
Dog-tired we have come back to the camp again. Our walk today took us to a beautifully picturesque area, the road covered over by a leafy roof of gigantic beech and oak; ivy as thick as an arm, and woodbine climbing up and around the heavy tree trunks. Now and then we could see through a gap in the bushes into a mysterious darkness, from which moss and grass-grown rocks were rising—and there—a glance into the beautifully blue distance and the sea glistening in the sunshine. After a bend in the road, a little brook embedded between beautiful wooded hills surprised us—now to be free! To be able to run down into the cool, purifying water! We stop for a little at the foot of a rock wall; happy people pass on bicycles,

in cars, with women and children. They don't know how fortunate they are.

July 13, 1945
Yesterday we were weighed. 60.5 kilo, I measured 168 centimetres.
Today I came across a Latin text and I was so glad that my translating still went so well. The familiar sounds of the language brought back school lessons with classmates and teachers, and behind it the spirit of that time 2,000 years ago, in the figure of a man whom I never before saw as I see him now. Today the air is so gentle and warm, and I still would like to take a few rounds along the barbed wire.

73ʳᴰ Mobile Field Bakery, Ruperra Castle

July 21, 1945
Since the 17th of July, we have been at this Field Bakery. For the first few days, I was the only interpreter.

Things didn't go this fast and smoothly. One day in Chepstow the word spread that they were looking for bakers. Amazing how many all of a sudden discovered that they were qualified for the job! They took a whole truckload of us on a curvy country road; we sat high enough so that we could look over the hedges at the pleasant landscape. Then along a wall and through a gate and there we were in front of a tall gray building that had seen better days. A sergeant major who was obviously in charge here asked whether any of us spoke English, and I volunteered. I translated the first basic instructions to take our things into one of the Nissen huts, where to stuff the palliasses, where we should assemble again for further instructions and when.

While the others scampered off, the Sergeant Major took me aside. He wanted to test my English for things to come. Said he, "You know 'dough'?", I said, "No." He did what many people in a situation like this do, he shouted: "Dough!" I still didn't under-stand. Why had we not learned that word in High School where they had always told us we were learning for life, not for the teachers? Was this the end of my interpreting? Of my staying in this nice place? He didn't give up but he did get irritated with this dense foreigner. Finally he shouted "Flower!" and when he added "Water" and made mixing motions I realized that he meant the other flour. *Teig!* That was it. Of course, we were in a bakery after all.

My trial wasn't over. I had to call the others into a big tent. We were lined up in front of a long camp table. There were clumps of that all-important dough on it and flour all over, and we had to show what we could do with it. I stood next to a heavy set fellow who could have been my father. He looked like a baker or any farmer who would bake his own bread. How could I ever hope to compete with him? But I could at least try to do what he was doing. He pulled that sticky mess off the table and then slapped it back down again, first from the one side, then from the other. I did the same thing but it didn't seem right; my neighbour began to sweat. After all, a lot depended on whether we made the grade or not. We might be sent back to that awful, crowded, boring camp in Chepstow or stay here where the country was so nice and where, the word bakery promised it, the food would have to be better, at least ampler. What a chance! We had to win. We dug our fingers into the mess, squeezed it until our knuckles got white, no use. It wouldn't shape up to anything. And all the time the Sergeant Major was watching us. We looked at him trying to read our fate in his face. That he didn't laugh or even crack a smile said a lot about the kind of man he turned out to be.

Thank God, they needed not only bakers. The fellow next to me also stayed on though I never found out what Fritz actually did, and I who had failed just as miserably, was considered useful after all, as an interpreter, as the second interpreter. Number one must have come a few days later. He was the German equivalent of the Sergeant Major; he knew his English, was efficient, neat, and spoke with a voice used to giving orders.

July 21, 1945.
The nicest thing here is the beautiful country around us with a view of the Bristol Channel where we can even see the ships in the distance–the old burnt-out castle–the wooded hills and no barbed wire. When we arrived here, we imagined we were in a fairyland. But then we had to put three rolls of barbed wire around our Nissen huts. Very valuable, too, is the conversation with the English personnel who are extremely friendly to us, and important is the good food! –That certainly was a quick change last Tuesday. Now we feel already at home here! How long are we going to stay???

August 2, 1945
Now we really are at home here. I am taking care of the bread delivery in the morning when the army trucks come to pick it up.

The bakers had been up long before us. When we got up, the bread was already in the cooling tent. It was baked in sets of six loaves, not round but rectangular with a nice rounded crust. These sets stood upright on their long side in the racks, and I had to count off the order for each of the trucks that came to pick them up to deliver them to various British and American army

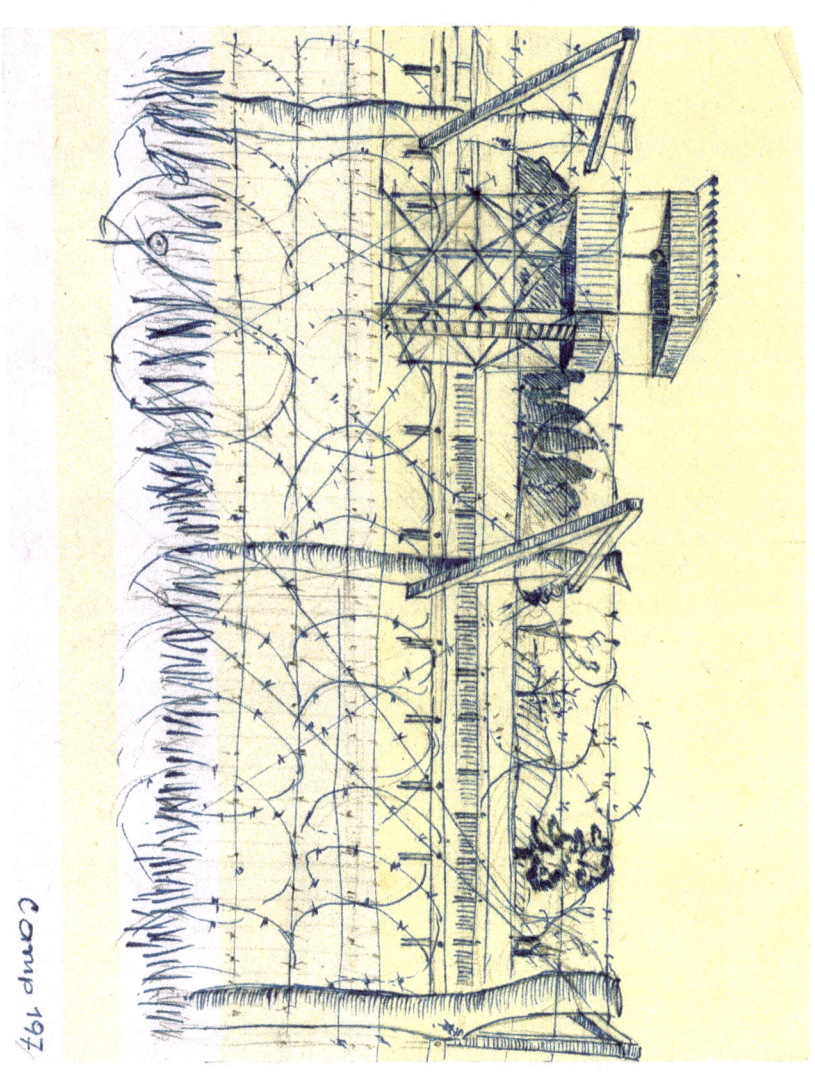

Camp 197- Sketch by H. Jarka

posts in the vicinity, one of them in Abergavenny. The rumour was that Rudolf Hess had been held there, but he had not eaten the bread we baked. He had left for Nuremberg before we came to Ruperra.

I am in charge of the bookkeeping of the flour and yeast supply all by myself. Did I have an awful mess yesterday: maggots had got into the yeast!

I doubt that I was actually in charge of all supplies needed in the bakery. But there I was in my little store room and there were sacks of flour leaning in the corner. Maybe it was the supply just for our kitchen needs.

The maggots were just one of my problems. At first the Sergeant Major had to correct all my "sevens" which I, in good European style, had crossed so that to him they looked as if they had been crossed out, and could cause all sorts of trouble which bookkeepers are prone to. One day he corrected an entry according to which we ought to have had one bag of flour more than we actually had. There was a short argument with the Sergeant. I never found out whether I had added up wrong or whether that one bag had just disappeared and he knew where it had gone. Actually I can't imagine him doing anything improper; he was too regulation bound. His skin was pink, his moustache red and always trimmed, his pants were always pressed, his shoes sparkled, his wide leather belt looked brand new. He was well fed, he was too stocky to be the perfect figure, but he was the model Sergeant Major. Not really a bad sort, but he had no humour that I could discover in that long year. But I think he liked me in his stiff way. He came into my little store room with a plate of cakes and said, "Would you like one?" and when I said, "Why not," he reprimanded me: "That's not the thing to say. You say 'Yes, please.'" I learned something every day.

Also about the soldiers' politics. We had not been at Ruperra for very long when one day there was a commotion in the courtyard. The soldiers were driving their little army truck wildly around in a circle honking all the time, and in the back behind the cab stood a skinny little fellow, Taffy, waving his arms and giving the "V" sign and shouting jubilantly: "Winston's out! Winston's out!" And on the truck roared, round and round. From a corner the Sergeant Major was watching, He looked grimmer than ever. Without saying a word, he disappeared. The overjoyed Labourite was Taffy. He was one of the guards, a Private, always joking with us and cheerful. I got to know him better than any of the others who were guards and not bakers.

Today again what a beautiful day. Blue sky and real summer sunshine. This morning I was up walking in the park at six o'clock. It's always so marvellous in the early morning when an untouched quietness surrounds the country in its veils of fog–or in the evening, when the first stars appear in the ocean of sky, twinkling gently, and the tops of the tall trees, together with the gigantic towers of the castle, are flooded by the sunlight of the passing day. —Then the gnarled pine trees, in their melancholy, seem to admonish me: you are having it good, but do you know how fate is playing with them who loved so much to listen to the wind in the trees with you at home? The wind in the eternal trees is like a bridge back to past days, but through their branches the all-embracing eternity of the stars is shining, which, again and again, makes me feel the nothingness of our lives.

Morning and evening were my time. I soon overcame the three loose rolls of barbed wire and explored the Castle grounds, a former park but now neglected and dreamy, no lawn, only tall wavy grass. There was a stone wall all around but it wasn't forbidding because higher and lower tops alternated like merlons and crenels, and I could always see the hill beyond and the Channel in the distance. There was a gate to the southwest, and through it I could see the meadows outside and a tree here and there. That gate with its stone vases on each pillar must have been the main entrance. From it the driveway led up to the imposing entrance with its wide steps and balustrades. The driveway was overgrown. Only the cedars and the gorgeous pink and white rhododendrons were left of the old glory and elegance of past receptions and garden parties. We were the only guests. There were rhododendrons in my home town, but only in the gardens of the rich, and I had never seen them close up. And cedars I had only read about.

There was another gate on that side of the wall, a padlocked utility gate of rusty round bars that promised an easier escape, but it could be seen from the castle buildings. Still that corner of the ground was more secluded, and I gravitated towards it. There was a pond with rotten leaves at the edges, and the tall trees made evening come sooner. I often waited there for the night, dreaming, and sometimes I would come into the Nissen hut and hurriedly write down a poem. Already in other camps I had started jotting down some verses, as escape from the crowds. Ruperra was the perfect atmosphere for writing more. These verses were in German of course and were originally for me only; I had read too much, copied too many poems, and thought too little, because poetry was supposed to be about feelings, wasn't it? Mine certainly was, full of soul-searching. That autumn the trees around the pond were my companions and my audience; they had to listen to my half-loud pleas and yearnings. I humanized them, I heard them whisper to each other. They were my models, they would help me rise from the dark undergrowth of my confusion to the freedom of tree tops where there was nothing but rustling and feeling. And the clouds, of course, how I travelled with them eastwards, always eastwards. The weather would write these verses, the sunshine of hope and the fog of doubt, the rain of self-pity. It was all a wonderful willed escape as my first lines in English said:

> The realist that I was forced to be
> Was by the night wind driven out of me...

Considering my "realism," the wind did not have to blow very hard.

Soldiers billeted in the castle had accidentally started a fire that gutted the inside and weakened the walls. There was a wide crack in one of the towers. The building was condemned, and we were not allowed to enter it. There were a number of service buildings where the personnel for the castle had lived and worked, and there the soldiers had their billets and the Sergeant Major his office. There were utility sheds and a garage and so on. And in one of these side buildings I had my little room with the stores and my ledger. There were even a few books in there, a token soldiers' library also open to us paws. But the soldiers never borrowed a book and the other POWs did not or did not want to read English, and I was the only patron of this educational facility. It was there that I read *Great Expectations*, in a fine clothbound edition with colour illustrations—in my memory Miss Havisham has been sitting surrounded by cobwebs ever since. The Dickens was the only major relatively modern work of any length that I read at Ruperra. I don't think there were any other similar books in that "library." One volume I took a liking to was Arthur Poyser's *The Tower of London* dedicated to the Boy Scouts as an aid to study for the King's Scout Badge, the holder of which must know "The History of an Ancient Building," London 1916. It had seen better days and was fortified with wide, black electrician's tape, but the print was good and the watercolour illustrations were almost idyllic, not a corpse anywhere. But there also was some poetry in the book which I copied to qualify the peacefulness of the pictures:

> The screw may twist and the rack may turn,
> And men may bleed and men may burn.
> On London town and all its hoard
> I keep my solemn watch and ward!

The Yeomen of the Guards

Oh yes, English history was gruesome, indeed. I am sure that the first two lines did not make me think of the horrors in German concentration camps. My repression of the film we had seen in Chepstow worked too well. English history, as it attracted my interest in the Tower of London, beckoned in a third book on the lonely shelf next to yeast and flour: Everyman's edition of *Shakespeare's Historical Plays, Poems and Sonnets*. I don't believe I read the book at the time, not even the "Rape of Lucrece" that might have promised erotic language, but this battered Shakespeare looked interesting. From a faintly legible black stamp on the front cover one could make out that the book had been in an Active Service Army School, and a red rubber stamp inside said "Army Forces Depot. W. York R. Sept. 1925. Part-Worn." Indeed, it seems to have been in many hands not always clean. There were dried grease stains all over it; perhaps a soldier had read it while cleaning his rifle. The book obviously had its own history, arid I was to add to it in my way.

Of course, I wasn't in my little realm all day, but I don't remember anything of the rest of the day and very little of my fellow POWs at Ruperra. We all got along well; there were no ugly conflicts as in the other camps. They were all very friendly to me. Some were a lot older than I was and might have thought of their own son when they saw me. Our group was coherent but had different schedules. I don't know any more what kind of work each of the others did. I don't remember much of the baking tent with the big mixer in it. I don't remember even where we had our meals, who made them and what they were. We had plenty to eat, and food, usually topic number one in the other camps, had lost its topicality. I have to strain my memory to see the faces of our group at Ruperra, and only a few appear before me dimly and with hardly any associations. There was Anton, the only baker that I recall. He was a friendly, chubby fellow with a shiny round face like a loaf. He always looked as if he had just come out of the oven. When he talked about his family he was always close to tears. And there was an elementary school teacher with an impressive head of hair. There was the non-baker Fritz who had failed the kneading test beside me: I saw him coming out of a prayer meeting one Sunday and said: "Fritz, I didn't think you were religious?" And he said with a sly wink: "I'm not, but you never know!" One younger fellow with curly blond hair spoke with a Rhinelander's lilt; he was always cheerful and raved about his favourite soccer team at home. With Paul, the forester, I spent more time than with anybody else, but try as I might I cannot remember his face anymore than that of any of the others who loaded bread with me every morning. Other faces may emerge as I go on writing this.

What did we do in our spare time together? Very soon we must have

Ruppera Castle - Sketch by H. Jarka, July 29, 1945

disregarded those loose rolls of barbed wire and ventured out to the grass around the castle. One Sunday afternoon we sat under the shady tree on the east side of the castle and one of us, a kind elementary teacher with a beautiful head of graying hair, led us in singing; nobody was interested in those army songs we had had to roar on fatigue marches and which, I understand, are still being roared at veterans' beer parties today. We sang folk songs one could not march to; the well known "Kein schöner Land zu dieser Zeit" –"No more beautiful land than ours," or one I had not known and have not heard since: "Saß einst im Kreise der Lieben" –"Long ago I was with my loved ones." I can hear the tune, and it brings back that afternoon in Ruperra. This teacher seemed to feel responsible for our emotional health, and that afternoon he hinted in some fatherly, advisory sense at our sexual needs which at night the creaky bedsteads might have betrayed. Did they put something in our food? Or not always enough?

What I remember most vividly was not our communal life in the camp, but what I discovered outside of it. All my longings for home, the dramatic, overstated self-pity belongs to the journal as is properly included here. But those emotions are gone now. What has stayed with me is what happened outside the camp: in the Welsh countryside, those one or two square miles on the Rhymney, and with the few Welsh people I met. And while I never even tried to keep in touch with my fellow POWs at Ruperra, I corresponded with my Welsh friends until they passed away one after the other.

August 9, 1945
Between the gaps in the wall and over it we saw the countryside but no people. Our main contact with the outside world was the drivers who came to pick up the bread in the morning. They were outsiders to me, but since they were in uniform they were only outsiders within that big community that unites all soldiers, enemy and friend. That union was not always felt, and in one case, at least the enemy was "the enemy," or acted like one in a surly, moody way. He was a stout fellow, dark haired and never friendly. He never talked to me or any other POW. While we were loading the bread he would lean with his left hand against the side of the truck while his right hand fumbled around with his fly, and he finally relieved himself on the back tire. We only called him the "tire pisser." I saw his face, or rather his type of head again, years later in the Welsh National Museum in Cardiff: right in the lobby there was a portrait. There he is, the tire pisser, I thought. "Welsh Miner" it was called. And it was only a very general likeness, the shape of the head, the

dark hair and eyebrows, but the miner's face was open, and he looked straight at me, something the tire pisser had never done.

And there was the other driver, tall, a bit heavy, gentle and very friendly. I remember quite vividly that morning when I was sick in bed with a fever, and somebody else had to count the six-packs of loaves onto the truck, and the tall heavy driver came in and sat on my bed and hoped I would get better soon. He probably thought of his own children and remembered that the Nissen hut wasn't my real home. I knew he had children for he bought them some products of our little POW craft industry that we bartered for cigarettes. Some drivers did not need anything in return for their cigarettes, or so we thought. Black GI's would often leave a pack of Lucky Strike on the back of their heavy US Army truck which we found when we loaded. We liked to think that they had left them for us, but whether they were gifts of kindness or carelessness, we accepted them without asking questions. In general, black soldiers were considered especially easy going. In the POW-camps in Belgium they were supposed to help POWs to get away by holding up the barbed wire for them. The black GIs that came to Ruperra were definitely more laid back than the Tommies entrusted with our care.

One scene sticks out in my memory. One morning a black guy asked us for help. He had a German army pistol in his hand and wondered about its workings. Soon a whole group of us stood around him and tried to enlighten him by taking the pistol apart. The lively chatter must have caught the attention of the Sergeant Major. To see a German POW with a pistol in his hand was not a sight he cherished, nor did he approve of American casualness. I don't think that GI was very impressed with the Sergeant's tirade, and we enjoyed it behind his back.

The ninth of August! My thoughts fly back to last year, when, on this day, I suddenly stood in front of Mother in the factory in my battle regalia and then went home in civies. How beautiful those days were. A leave-taking for a few months, as we thought, and now a whole year has gone by and I'm spending my twentieth birthday at an old hunting castle of some Lord in Wales. Only one year, but so full of events and changes inside me and around me. I know that today you are all thinking of me—if you are still alive! Do I dare to look ahead? Where shall I find myself a year from now?

August 11, 1945
My journal, it's a year today that I left home with you in my soldier's tunic. It was just as hot a sunny day as it is today and home appears again in front of my eyes with its last

impressions. Goodbye from Mother with a smile—I'll be back in three months: and then with Ruth to the station and the familiar train to the city. Goodbye Kahlenberg, goodbye Danube! Then the common experience of the departure at the West Station made the final jump easier. Starry night! Moonlight floods the roads which evoke memories: do you remember? And then into the strangeness—France, destruction, desolation—hopeless existence behind barbed wire.

August 14, 1945

Yesterday, most of the English crew were transferred. Only a few are left. Although they were Englishmen, enemies, I'm sorry that they're leaving. It always was so much fun to chat with Corporal Ernie Freeman in the bakery. How often we have laughed together, and wrestled together. Above all, I learned so much English from him, which was very valuable. Staff Sergeant Gibbs, too, is gone, who was so friendly from the first day. But Horst! What are you saying? Enemies!

Did I write this because I thought that was the way I should feel? How much of my journal was dictated by a soldier's obligation and manipulated responses? Of course, the guards in the previous camps were "enemies," and not people; they were simply enemy uniforms with machine pistols on guard towers or behind barbed wire and provoked or unprovoked would swear at us, except when some bargaining transaction necessitated a more neutral, if not friendly, exchange of words. I never did any bargaining, and had no personal contact at all. But the soldiers at Ruperra were different; they were the only English soldiers I met who actually talked with us.

August 18, 1945

Yes, there is something strange about this meeting with the English. It's so valuable to look into the inside of these people, whom one imagines so cool and reserved, and who suddenly show themselves so completely as human beings with the same worries that we have, as they told us of their wives and children and the air raids. Once I spent two and half hours with Staff Sergeant Gibbs, lying in the grass in front of the castle: he showed me his pictures, pulled out the wad of money he has saved to buy something that will make his wife happy, and how much he wished that everything would be ok with my loved ones when I got home. Why this damned war! !?—or was the attitude of the Tommies so friendly because they themselves had never been at the Front?

They may not have seen "action," but in the second World War the "Home Front" was also a front at home. The air raids that the soldiers talked about could have justified any animosity towards us, but they showed none. Staff Sergeant Gibbs—or was it Corporal Eccles?—did not have to correct my English compositions nor did he have to buy for me a booklet on Star

Recognition because I was interested in astronomy. Why did I feel I had to qualify friend-liness?

Only a few of the soldiers were connected with the bakery itself. I would chat and goof off with them in the big tent with the bread making machinery in it. And a few others were guards to see that nobody ran off with the equipment, and that we wouldn't run off ourselves. We hardly ever saw the soldiers in a group together, and the two army songs I remember from Ruperra –, "There are rats, rats, as big as bloody cats in the store, in the quartermaster's store," and "Roll me over in the clover"–I probably learned from Taffy, the liveliest of them all. In the evening the soldiers silently disappeared to a pub in Machen, or the movies. In the morning they would emerge–from the beds in their Ruperra quarters or from some other beds, who knows? We never felt very much watched–or supervised, except by the Sergeant Major. All the other soldiers seemed to be on light duty, waiting to be demobbed. At the beginning an officer dropped by occasionally in a sort of embarrassed, perfunctory way as if checking up on a field bakery had never been the goal of his ambition. He was a slight man with a pale nervous face and black-rimmed glasses, a civilian in uniform, who lived with his wife in private billets round a few bends down the road. One day he was gone, and nobody missed him.

August 26, 1945
After a long rainy time, finally a marvellous, laughing summer day.
Yes, it was a sunny summer day just like that, when exactly two years ago, I said goodbye at home and joined the army. When I in shorts, suitcase in hand, stood in Ruth's room and waited for her to get ready, and when, from the small radio, the melody came "In the cornfield, the red poppies glow."

October 1, 1945
One year a POW. A year full of hope of an end and here I am still in England without any news from home. During the last few days we had a lot of work and so the bakery helps us not to think too much. In Camp 1 in Chepstow, some of us have already been repatriated, supposedly only those born before 1900. I myself expect at least another year before we younger ones can even think about getting home.

October 12, 1945
I was just back in camp and I've heard that Gerhard Wuster is going home on Tuesday. Too bad that I couldn't see him anymore. I quickly wrote him a letter. Perhaps we can see

each other again at home.

Our fame was spreading, at least that of our confectioner. One day to our surprise a couple of officers from some army post arrived and ordered a fancy cake for some special occasion, a wedding, a medal, a promotion or something, and they brought all the ingredients: sugar and butter, or was it still margarine and honey and various jams. And these ingredients, especially when stretched a bit, proved so ample that there was always enough left over for some goodies for us. So, in absentia, we too celebrated the officers' function and gorged ourselves with German pastries. And we appreciated our confectioner's skill as much as the officers who came back again and again. After all, our delightful products were not only of continental quality, they were also cheap.

No journal entries all November. That must have been the time when I could not write. For transporting bags of flour we used heavy two wheel carts with a T-shaped handle, and, putting the cart away in the shed, my right hand got caught between handle and wall. One finger was badly hurt; the nail was pushed out of the nail bed. One of the guards took me immediately to the doctor in Machen down in the Rhymney Valley. I had been to the doctor before in the camps, but those were army doctors and the patients POWs. Nothing new. But this was different! I was going to a regular doctor in a small town in Wales. As we entered the waiting room a few patients—all civilians!—were looking at us as all patients look at newcomers. But I had a soldier at my side; I was special, I thought. The patients soon looked away again, and returned to their own pains and ills, just like patients at home. My finger healed soon, only the tip of it turned out flatter than the other fingers, and the new nail rounder. It still is like that, a lasting souvenir of Ruperra.

Another reason for the gap in my journal might have been that it was the first time when I managed to borrow a typewriter. Already in the other camps I had begun to copy by hand German poems, snatches of literary histories, even a whole play, in no particular order; it probably depended on what I could get. From where? I don't remember where all these German texts came from. Camp libraries, personal copies some soldiers had brought with them? Red-Cross shipments? No matter, I covered page after page, to fill the time, to remember familiar poems, to be home again in verses once memorized. Now I had a typewriter! And did I copy now! Hugo's "To Voltaire," a scene from *Faust*, from Goethe's aphorisms by the dozen, and above all, Rilke. One of the young fellows in the bakery had a Rilke edition. The fellow was not really arrogant, but somehow thought of himself as made of different stuff.

He was vain and very careful of his black Panzer jacket with pink piping. His rich black mane was always clean and styled as if he had a date every night. Of all the boys there he was the one to have secured a copy of the early Rilke with *The Cornet* in it, that orgy of romantic love, war and beauty, and the *Books of Hours*. I copied it all and must have given him the original typescript because I have only the carbons. I didn't understand Rilke's mysticism but that was just as well. The melodiousness of his lines, the singsong of the rhymes, held an intoxicating fascination for me. I memorized incantations in the *Book of Hours* and I still know them:

> Ich lebe mein Leben in wachsenden Ringen,
>   I live my life in growing rings
> Die sich über die Dinge ziehn,
>   Circling over every thing,
> Ich werde den letzten vielleicht nicht vollbringen,
>   The last one I may not reach
> Aber versuchen will ich ihn
>   But attempt it I will.

Rilke's mystical soliloquies touched a chord in me, who liked to lose himself in the eternity of moon and stars and wind and the clouds way up beyond the swaying treetops.

There is one poem I wrote that autumn that tells its own romantic story of another clandestine adventure. I wanted to explore more than that pond, and my curiosity turned me north. The wall was higher there, but at the inside corner there were some cracks with loose mortar, and I could inch my way up to look over the top. There was the road that we had come on that first day. I looked both ways, then jumped down onto the asphalt and across, and the darkness beyond swallowed me up. It was a dense wood of fairly young conifers, spruces maybe. I pressed on through the scratchy dry lower branches and soon found myself on a path, thick with needles, not very wide and beginning to get narrower from disuse, and up it went. It was so quiet and the air was sweet with the scent of the trees. I walked quickly, curious to see where it all ended. I came to a knoll at last with a wall of large stones around it. Some were loose, and I scrambled up to a kind of kiosk made of the same trees that I had walked through; there was a roof over it and the sides were open. I could see in all directions between the tops of the highest trees. It was getting dark fast and I couldn't see the trees below, nor the castle or anything nearby, only a few lights in the distance. Slowly the moon rose. I stood entranced, looking at the sky, and the wind came up.

> *All around me surging sea of treetops*
> *Rocking in the foamy moonlight.*
> *On a dark path I stormed the summit.*
> *Now, deep below me the light of men...*
> *The world sunk deep in silver haze,*
> *The cold wind a greeting from freedom so far away*
> *The soul is drunk with its strength*
> *And dissolves...*

...naturally.

December 7, 1945
Today I found out that I am allowed to write to Vienna. After an interruption of many months.

My last card was dated March 28. We could write again! What a relief I sent one of those POW-cards of seven lines, my first card since the end of the war:

> Dear Mother, Dear Ruth:
> Finally I can send you a sign of life again. I am doing fine, am working in a bakery as an interpreter. I hope you are well. Perhaps these lines will cheer you up at Christmas! Give Ilse my regards.
>
> Kisses, Horst

From this card they knew at least that I had enough to eat. I wonder what Mother thought when she saw that card. She herself, as a POW in 1918 when her field hospital had been taken over by the Italians, had sent such a card home.

Christmas was approaching and our POW home industry went into high gear. A piece of one inch soft wood would be carved into a bird's head on one side, and the other side would be spliced into thin layers which very carefully could be fanned out to make a tail, and a cross piece fanned into wings. The whole bird would be decorated with a simple design burnt in with a glowing piece of wire. I remembered that Russian POWs had made these kinds of toys in this international POW-folk art tradition.

But we at Ruperra had also something else to offer, something unique. Thanks to Lord Tredegar and the solid good taste with which he had

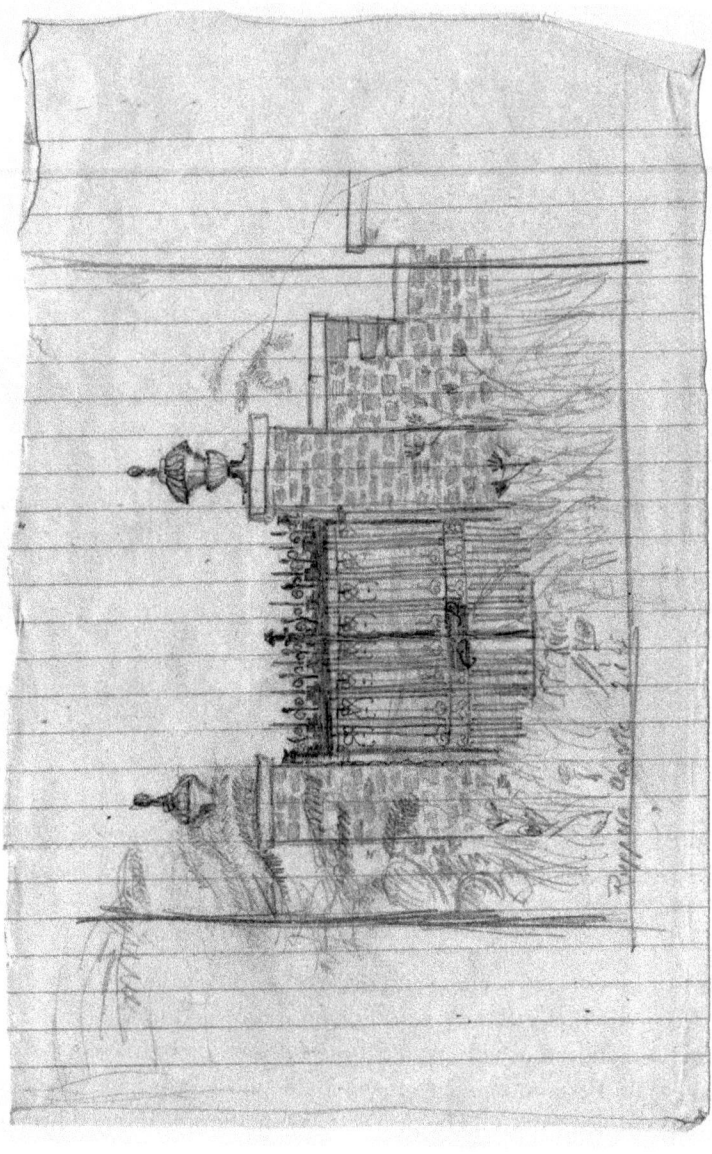

Ruperra Castle - The Garden Gate of Ruperra Castle from the Inside.
Sketch by H. Jarka, January 2, 1945.

furnished his castle, and thanks to the British soldiers who had burned it down or at least demolished it enough to make it useless—useless to others—nothing is useless to a POW. Of course we were not supposed to get inside the castle; it was condemned, but we had seen worse ruins, and we ventured forth. As I was stoking around in the ashes one day, something shiny caught my eye: One of those dainty, ladies' opera glasses, the little eye-pieces and all sides covered with mother of pearl. The heat had blinded one of the bigger lenses, and its little counterpart was missing. The brass casing was dull, but after I had cleaned it the delicate relief design that ran around the big lenses was perfect, and the mechanism still worked. I treasured it, and still have it. How I ever got it through all the searches, I don't know. Maybe I had given it to Ernie, and he sent it after me. I could have had it repaired years ago but somehow its imperfection preserves its charm. Looking through the one good lens, I wish I could see the elegant lady who had taken the glass to Ruperra. When? To view what? What entertainment had Ruperra offered? Concerts? Perhaps even plays? And hadn't she missed it? Had it been too late to retrieve it? Had those careless soldiers already moved in and dropped their cigarettes allover the place?

Other scouts were rewarded with more prosaic bounty, treasures none the less: some oak panelling, of just the right thickness, which had somehow survived the fire, and some especially valuable brass sheeting. I don't remember where that came from, possibly from the trim of the several fireplaces in the building where the Lord's sporting guests had warmed themselves after the hunt, and exchanged their toasts and tall tales. We hammered the metal, then blackened it, wiped off the excess, so that the rims between the hammer marks would be clean and could be polished. With its pattern of black and gold, the metal provided quite handsome lids and sides to the oak boxes we had made. They fetched a good price in cigarettes from the drivers and the Newport or Cardiff locals who, on a weekend outing, would come to gawk at the Germans, and bargain with them through the wrought-iron bars of the park gate.

December 10, 1945

Dear Mother, Dear Ruth!

The days are cold. The first snow is powdering the trees which have become my companions. Winter is upon us, as at that time when I first wrote to you. A year full of difficult days has passed since, and still no news from you. Time raced by and the last days at home

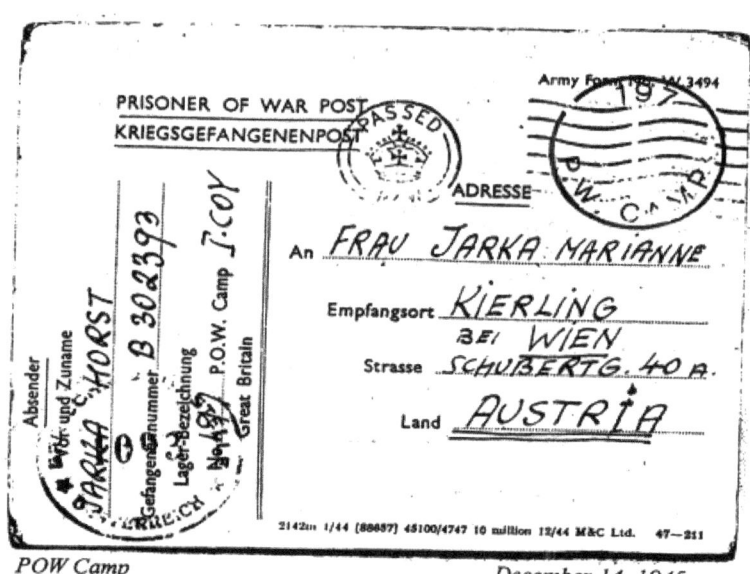

POW Camp   December 14, 1945

Dear Mother, dear Ruth!
I hope that news from me will finally reach you. I am waiting for mail every day. I feel fine, am in good health and only wait to hear the same of you. Many kisses Horst

seem to drown in the grey fog of this country. But how often does the past become present when the wind goes through the pines and when the same stars move across the sky. Observing nature, I learn to look deeper into it and to enjoy its eternity. The opportunity to speak English has helped me a great deal and the easy work in the bakery chases the hours. Now that so many comrades have received mail from home, I can't stop questioning and hoping. How are you doing? Are you still where I left you? And the food? How happy I would be to know that you live as well as I do. You can really rest assured, at last I can write and another letter goes out into the uncertainty accompanied with all my wishes that it may find you. Again, the forest is Christmasy and again I let my thoughts fly on the snow clouds that are moving east to you.

December 25, 1945

Second Christmas behind barbed wire. Mild, rainy weather as I take my walk. Isn't it strange that this time Christmas doesn't touch me as much? Is it because this year we're celebrating more in style and not as miserably as last year? Is it because the spring-like weather prevents a true Christmas spirit, even if the candles are burning on the tree. Or is it Time that has our heart in its grip and doesn't allow our feelings to express themselves?

There was less emotion in that Christmas, maybe that's what I missed, being used to the quiet, if you will, sentimental German family Christmas. We had a kind of English Christmas party with laughter and kidding; in the merriment I must have forgotten my melancholy gloom because, being the only Viennese in the group, I entertained by crooning schmaltzy songs, and everybody clapped and gave me candy.

December 26, 1945

Dear Mother and dear Ruth, [...] After our celebration I withdrew to the woods and was alone. I like being alone. I wonder how you spent these days? Did you have enough bread while I was eating cake? Who knows in what cold hole you had to celebrate the festival of peace while we were sitting in a warm hut listening to the radio. I hope you're both together and well. As I am writing to you, I see both of you and everything at home as it was in August of '44. But how everything can have changed! And this uncertainty often comes over me with a terrible force. I can't even think about how everything used to be. I've now tried to find something out about you through acquaintances. No answer yet. But I still have hope, so goodbye.

Now I'm standing on my beloved lookout hill: deep down the sea is shining with a copper glow through the veils of fog.

January 1, 1946
The New Year's bells are fading that the wind had carried us to Newport and Cardiff. Ships' sirens are howling and now and then a big bang—but Mars and Saturn stand unmoved in the zenith. Infinitely far back is the time when I celebrated the last New Year at home and toasted a happy 1944. Was it a happy year?

Something happened about that passage from 1945 to 1946 which, if it happened when I assume it did, must have put the melancholy I recorded in my journal in a very different perspective. I am not sure about the sequence of events but it sounds probable enough to me now. One morning, as we were loading the bread, we noticed to our horror pieces of glass sticking out of the appetizing crisp crust of some of the loaves! Had we already loaded some of that dangerous stuff? And what had happened? And were we the first ones to discover the catastrophe? The unthinkable had happened: in the huge mixing machine the glass thermometer, about a foot long had been forgotten in the dough, and the powerful arm that turned and turned the mass as in a huge washing machine had mixed the pieces in. And all that mercury! I don't know whether the baker on duty that morning had gone back to bed or what, and how on earth the process had gone on unnoticed to the point that we found the glass in the cooled loaves I don't remember. Or had there been more mixing, and had it happened only in one batch? What a pernicious act of sabotage that could have been–if the war had been still on and if we had not eaten the bread ourselves–and if bakers were by nature saboteurs. I wasn't there when the Sergeant Major found out; I can only imagine his fury. But actually nothing happened along that line, and if anybody was blamed, nobody was dismissed and sent back to Chepstow. But more bread had to be turned out for all those hungry soldiers still waiting for their breakfast, and there was all that "spiked" bread, what a waste.

But was it all wasted? There was a small farm in the neighborhood and regularly Mr. Thomas the farmer came by to pick up our garbage. He was a slight man in a little truck that pulled a makeshift two-wheel trailer with a barrel on it, dripping with swill. Mr. Thomas was quiet and unobtrusive, almost shy, as if collecting the garbage was a special privilege granted by the

Lord of Tredegar himself. There was, at least in my imagination, something of a feudal dependency about it all; perhaps his status made him especially sympathetic to us underdogs in patched uniforms. Thomas certainly was the only civilian I had met in Ruperra so far. He loaded quite a few of our dangerous loaves of bread on his truck to dump it somewhere? Or did he salvage some of it, pullout the bits of glass and feed the bread to his pigs? Or had not all loaves been spoiled and had to be thrown out just to be safe? The whole episode with the glass in the bread was the most exciting thing that had happened so far, and we spun it out in surmises and guesses.

There was more excitement to come, and Mr. Thomas had a leading part in it. His weekly visits had established a certain bond of familiarity with us. I never saw him talking with the soldiers; they were not even around when he came. He got the garbage from us, not them. So one day there he came trudging up to us in his dirty Wellies, and in his arms he carried, tried to carry a squirming young pig for us! A New Year's gift? A token of his appreciation for all that garbage, a simple gesture of friendliness? But it was for us, for our kitchen. I don't remember anything about our kitchen. I know we had our own cook and our own meals. I don't remember whether the guards ate with us; if so they were probably grateful for a European touch in the British Army regulation fare. So here was this pig, and we did not tell anybody about it, certainly not the Sergeant Major. Where could we keep our precious gift till we were ready for its slaughter? There was only one place to hide it: in the cellar of the castle. It was out of sight of the guards and the Sergeant Major. There were partitions down there for storing firewood and other supplies; they were made of tall narrow slats; they were airy and safe. And that's where we put our treasure, and to keep piglet happy we pushed greens through the slats. It was all very secretive and exciting. What a meal we were looking forward to: real juicy pork chops, pork roast, and bacon!

We were filling the bathtub with steaming water. Everything was ready for the slaughter. And then all the secrecy and the dream collapsed in squeals and screams and commotion; everybody, soldiers and POWs, were running around in the courtyard chasing the common enemy. The pig had not liked the darkness and felt trapped, and maybe it was homesick and wanted to get out. It had gnawed through those soft-wood slats and gained freedom. We should have sympathized with it and felt happy that it was free. But we chased our pork roast and bacon. The pig was very fast and outmaneuvered us all for a while. Then we finally cornered the squealing creature and tied its legs. What now? There was quite a discussion. The soldiers took our side and argued that there was no harm in accepting the gift and eating it together. The Sergeant Major, however, was firm. He would never permit it; he couldn't. It was against regulations. But we would never tell anybody. No. The strict war-time regulations governing slaughter were still in effect. Everybody, including Mr. Thomas, would be in serious trouble. The pig had to be returned. Thomas was sorry it had not worked out for us. To protect our well-meaning donor, I did not record the incident in my journal. Who knows who might have read about it? It was probably illegal to give presents to POWs, especially piglets. That was a feast we missed.

January 9, 1946
The wind is howling around the barracks and the rain is whipping the trees. Behind the chasing clouds the waxing moon. Your birthday.

> *Dich sah ich, und die milde Freude*
> I saw you and a gentle joy
> *Floß aus dem süßen Blick auf mich.*
> Flowed from your sweet glance to me.
> *Ganz war mein Hertz an deiner Seite*
> My heart was on your side,
> *Und jeder Atemzug für dich....*
> And every breath was for you...

(Goethe)

January 12, 1946
On the 11th letter to Mother and Ruth: "And isn't our whole existence nothing but a hiding in the past or a hope rarely free from torturing doubts?" A few new comrades have joined us, a forester with whom I now want to study botany.

January 30, 1946
I've just written another letter to Mother, for the first time not sent out into uncertainty. Yes, this morning, Scholz brought me a letter from Mother to the bread tent. How much your letter is worth to me, Mother! It's the most precious possession that I have. You are alive! Now there is a future. Nothing can hold me back. And Ilse visited Mother. She's going to the university. Yes, I too want to go there. It must be possible. I can hardly believe it yet, and I'm so happy. These are Mother's words again, "Now all will be well." Now there is only one aim for my thoughts: home!!! At night the blackbirds are singing in the

dusk and pull me with them in their longing. At night, I can hardly fall asleep and would love nothing better than to get up and run to the east. Run and run, until I can finally sit down with Mother and rest. But in the morning it is always a cruel awakening to reality. Work helps a lot, and when the day comes to an end, the only good feeling is that it's been another day closer to home.

Der erste Brief

Wo kamst du her, du Gruß aus, ferner Welt
Die meine Seele klammernd in sich birgt,
Daß sie im Sturm der Zeiten nicht zerschellt?

Du kamst wie eine sanfte, zarte Hand,
Vor der die Qual des Irrens schwindet,
Die Hand, die immer meine Wunden findet
Und kühlend lindert meiner Sehnsucht Brand.

Du kamst aus jenen weiten Tiefen,
Woraus der Müde immer Ruhe trinkt,
Du warst ein Blick aus Augen, die mich riefen
von dort —wohin die Hand mich flehend winkt.

The first letter

Where did you come from,
greeting from a distant world
My soul's been holding in itself secure
Against the shattering storms of our times?

You came, a gentle tender hand
Making all doubt and torment vanish
The hand that always finds my wounds
And cooling stills my longing's fire.

You came from those distant depths
where tired souls drink peaceful rest,
You were a glance from eyes that call me
To where the hand is beckoning me to come.

I had not heard from home for a year and a half. I had been able to write

Ilse

in December 1944 to let them know that I was a POW and safe. Some of my mail did reach them. But I did not hear whether they had been exposed to bombing, whether they survived the fighting when the Russians took the town, and if they had survived and how they had been doing since. After the war Austria was divided into four occupation zones, and Klosterneuburg was occupied by the Russians. They knew that I had no news from home and frantically tried to establish contact. They had mailed letters in the British zone of occupation hoping that would speed things up, but it didn't help. Finally they sent a radio telegram which reached Newport on February 3, 1946, and a Red Cross Express Message that went to Camp 17, 189, and eventually 197 (Chepstow) which I received at the same time. From that time on the mail worked very well each way. All envelopes from Austria were opened; some were closed again with scotch tape and marked. MIL. CEN. CIVIL MAILS. Most were sealed with ordinary brown tape, but all letters inside were decorated with the purple rubber stamp of the Austrian censors who only once blacked out one word and cut out two others.

Once contact was established a letter would take at least three weeks in each direction, and, as in war time, a real correspondence was hardly possible.

For us POWs every letter was a treasure, every insignificant detail significant. I read every letter, every word again and again, and eagerly awaited the next mail day. Home was no longer a painful memory, the future no longer inscrutable. Censorship prevented details about critical times at the end of the war, but I learned the basics. Mother had stayed in Klosterneuburg with consequences she would not write about. Ruth had fled west before the Russians came, and was now living in the American zone; Ilse, too, had spent those weeks in the western part of Austria and was now back home.

As Mother herself wrote: all her letters were variations on the theme of the "longing to see you again," and that was always there, but what gave them her individual voice was the tension between realism and her longing to see me. She wanted me to be home, but told me not to hurry because home wasn't all that pleasant; there wasn't enough to eat. She was sad that men my age had come back and started college, and I had to stay behind, but she was glad that I could do some studying in that faraway country. She had had a hard life as a single mother, and hardship to her meant loyalty; looking forward to my return and a new beginning in the difficult times after the war, she wrote; "You always stuck with me through thick and thin; we'll just have to start all over again." There she was in her mid-fifties, sorry that she could not be with me in England, and that was not just a passing mood. Years later she emigrated with me to the States at the age of 72. And she predicted that my home country would be too small for me one day, and she even knew that one day I would treasure my time in Wales.

Here are some extracts from the first letters I received at the end of January:

Nov. 27, 1945

Son of my Heart!

How worried you must be about us! If a few things were different one could believe that we have peace. It's so peaceful to see the lighted windows [after the years of black-out] on this side of the valley and beyond. Ilse is going to the University studying German and Physical Education, Ruth is in the American zone, and I sit here and wait for my children. How we survived it all? Well, I am old now, and it took me 56 years to realize that the world, the whole world, not just ours, is a Punch and Judy show. Better late than never, and with this knowledge I will end my life. If you two come back healthy nothing can upset me any more. I am going to the factory as I always did. The roads and paths that we walked are the same. Only a few faces that one saw every day are missing. –A few graves on the wayside.– The one goes sooner, the other later. A few funny things spice the days. One does not see many boys your age; they all are going on with their studies and you are staying away so long.

January 27, 1946

Don't worry about us. Everything is as it used to be apart from some changes due to the times. I am guarding the house. I again sit all day at the sewing machine in the factory, only right now we are working nights because then the electric power supply is better. We have now electric lights here at home. What do you say to that achievement? [I had grown up with a kerosene lamp.]

Your Latin teacher is busy collecting sticks in the woods behind our place. We have had a rather severe winter…

To show why the letters were so much a part of my life, I would have to give them in full and all of them. I shall quote from them off and on to show how, in these direct links, home was always present as a close foil to the other impressions that made up my everyday life as a POW.

February 20, 1946
A short excursion to Cardiff. Taffy takes me with him to change brushes and brooms. Very nice drive. Rainbow. Sunshine. Castleton, Cardiff. Suburbs. Gasworks. City. Trams. And buses with double decks. University College. Clark College. Beautiful section of town. Civic Centre. Very beautiful monumental administrative buildings. Guild Hall. Technical College. Law Courts. Peace monument. Monument of the Unknown Soldier, 1914-18. Across from the Ministry of Justice, a building with a clock tower, is the Welsh National Museum. Monuments. Among them, the ancestor of the present owner of Ruperra Castle, Lord Tredegar on horseback. Taffy drove in a circle so that I could see as much as possible of the most beautiful part of town. Then the barracks of the Welsh Regiment. Very old-fashioned. And when I carried the basket with the brushes to the place where they changed them, I imagined I was in the Tower of London. I had also seen a high wall with towers and turrets that reared up behind it, but I don't know what it was. Striking was the white stone of which all the buildings of the Civic Centre are built. This part of town was built around the turn of the century and is supposed to represent the strongest contrast to the dark quarters which I also would very much like to see. On the drive back, beautiful view of the Channel.

February 22, 1946
Two letters from Mother. My card to my English teacher came back. Recipient deceased. My thanks came too late. Since I have mail from home, and from you, Ilse, a new period of my captivity has started. If it's possible at all to look back, then I see myself thus. At first hope, no answer from the other side, desperate hope, as if to force Fate. It can't be. Memories rise up with melancholy and hold me. No answer from over there. And now a slow process of separation. Time is pulling at the ties to the past. I'm looking up. A questioning, a looking, a premonition of the terrible mystery of the cosmos in which my self is drowning and finds peace. Moments of freedom and isolation, not of separation from the past, but a rising above it, drifting, where to? It is like a dream in which I tear myself away from reality which attacks me in the memories, which do not get away from us because they have become part of us. In the silence of uncertainty, they strike like the irony of Fate—the sudden rays of sun, flaming in my heart. A happy smile that lets me drop off my dreamy heights and wake up in warmth, which comes from over there. Memory becomes happy present and future. I'm standing on solid ground again. The earth has me again and grabs me and pulls me with longing, and again I ask, why so long? And again I'm looking into the darkness that quieted me, but now I'm not looking into emptiness. I find the eyes of home beaming at me. And you, Ilse, walking towards me.

March 2, 1946
Outside the wall stand seven dirty boys who strike up a conversation with me. One of them,

a blond devil, is their leader and with his thirteen years, he's learning Latin and wants to be a doctor one day. They absolutely want to have souvenirs from me. I think back to the time when, on the hikes one summer, I met Belgian and French prisoners of war and asked them for their buttons. And now I'm in the same position. But I'm happy to see them, these cheerful boys with their laughing eyes, the same eyes as the boys at home.

I don't remember whether I could fulfil their wishes. What did I have to give them? Buttons? Some of us wore German army jackets, whether our own or somebody else's that fit us better, or ones that were just thrown at us in one of the many check-ups and delousing stations. The fellow with his black tank corps jacket for instance thought so much of his good looks that he must have held on to his or adopted one that looked sharp. And Scholz did have some, probably his own, silver of authority on his collar edges. Whatever jackets we wore, they all had a big dark brown patch sown on in the back as the unmistakable sign of our status. Our other, though quite unobtrusive distinguishing mark was the mysterious arrow on our issue razors. Only years later when reading an illustrated edition of Oscar Wilde's *Ballad of Reading Gaol* did I realize that POWs had been given regular prison toilet, utensils, like murderers or thieves. How romantic. But we had our dignity.

One Sunday another group of young "visitors" strolled by. One lone straggler, a boy of twelve or so asked me shyly: "Please, Sir, do you know what time it is?" Sir! No one had ever called me Sir before! I pulled out my grandfather's pocket watch and told him. "Thank you, Sir." he said, and off he went.

March 8, 1946
Card to Mother: *To my indescribable joy I had seven letters from you, the latest of which is dated February 10.* This was the way the mail worked, in spurts.

February 2, 1946
Spring weather. Was in Vienna, and I walked from Sievering to Döbling past the Beethoven monument and the presbytery where he lived. All streets were empty. When will the pulse of life return to this city?

February 4, 1946
I'll tough it out, am waiting for you, and eat what doesn't eat me. The

main thing is that you are all right. Will the spring bring you into my arms?

February 5, 1946

Can you see your favourite star in England? Of course, why shouldn't you see it? I am looking for it every night and send greetings to you with it. The day will come when we look at the eternal stars together, and then I will be happy. When you were very little I was so happy when you were sleeping in your bed breathing quietly; then I would say very softly: "my son" as if this little word encompassed all sacred feelings. Sometimes I feel as if it were the biggest crime today to bring children into this brutal world. The most sacred feelings are being manipulated on demand. But this chapter is endless. So no more about it. I can't change things.

Feb. 10, 1946

We are waiting for you. If you're all right where you are you need not hurry to come home. You are not missing a thing here. Ilse says that the University is still just limping along. As far as we are concerned you need not worry at all. Everything is still where it used to be, just a little shabby.

Letter from Ilse:

Klosterneuburg, February 2, 1946

My dear Horst!

Am I writing these words to you or am I sending them out into a universe unknown to me? How far you are from me! The knowledge that you are alive and well makes us all very happy, but humans are immodest, and so I wish the hour were here when you will stand before me...If you could tell me all your thoughts and worries, how would I love to take part in your inner life. As it is, you are becoming a figure that I cannot reach in the hours of everyday life. A figure that is only near to me when I am alone and can send my thoughts awandering. Then it comes from far, far away and "brings with it pictures of happier days."

I am thinking of you often, but today I have the feeling that you are aware of it, as if we were together somewhere and talked with each other. Where is this place? A beautiful scene in nature, a musical masterpiece, a poetic creation—then I am with you, and we let the eternal beauty of the world sink into our hearts.

On the 6th I start a skiing course in Styria, and I will mail a letter to you in the British zone. Maybe you'll get it.

If the University didn't hold me, Vienna would not interest me; nothing but ruins and hunger.

March 10, 1946

Yesterday I was down at the pond again which I visit almost every day. It was dusk, and softly the birds were gliding through the chilling air. I have just read again Mother's and Ilse's letters when perhaps two yards from me a rabbit emerges from its hole. It sits and listens, then it sits up and looks at me with its brown wondering eyes. I am thinking of Rilke's lines. I am reading Scheffel's Ekkehard *which I like very much because he was a mystic or because I come across familiar passages like the story about the marmots, or is it because Ilse may be studying the same subject matter now?*

March 17, 1946

Yesterday, in our canteen, a discussion about faithfulness in marriage. Our side (Paul's and mine?): *What I expect of a woman I must keep myself! The other side, the soldiers who had been in France, that is: one must practice tolerance and also forgive the woman!! However, in this wisdom of experience of the two marriages, I always hear a great sadness over something lost or over something that was never found and a consolation with rationalizations. But since when is there reason in love? I'm reading now Hölderlin's* Hyperion. *Very beautiful.*

Dear Mother, March 21 1946

I am so happy to have received twelve letters from you already, and I am always so glad to feel our harmony in your words. Only when I see how strong your trust is, I always feel so small having given in to doubt and despondency. But you understand me. Did you not yourself write that card from a POW camp in Italy? After a few cold days it has become quite warm now, and the blackbirds are singing their longing out into the dying day. Around us spring is rising fragrant out of the ground. Between the tops of the cedars, the Bristol Channel is glistening and takes me back to the lakes at home—or is it luring me into distant lands? No, it still beckons in vain. Only to be home again!

My lost *Faust*? I got over that loss long ago—one of the lessons I've learned here: It is always best to keep such things where no one can take them from you.

April 5, 1946
To my great joy and surprise, I also received an English letter from the Soltoft family in Sweden. What wonderful people, who even after such a long interruption, have not forgotten and help again, as they did after the first World War, when I wasn't even born yet, and they sent food for Mother and Ruth. I want to write my next letter to them, and I'm looking forward to writing it in English.

April 7, 1946, Sunday
Marvellous morning. Got up at 5:00 and took a one hour outing avec velo. *Wonderful. I even saw a fox crossing the road.*

That must have been my first stealthy escape on the bike which I had "borrowed" from the guard house. I don't even know whether the soldiers actually slept there on weekends. They might have been billeted somewhere in the neighbourhood, and on Sunday we hardly ever saw them. But I felt daring, snitching one of their bikes. It was part of my unconscious game of secrecy and defying the rules in a morning of freedom.

Obviously, spring made me more adventurous. The bike I borrowed only at rare moments of daring, but around the castle grounds there were still huge white areas on my map that asked to be explored. One day I left that familiar pond and ventured farther through the trees and bushes, and suddenly was face to face with a middle-aged man out on a stroll like myself. What was I to do? I could not turn back. He was not unfriendly and quietly asked my name. Oh no! I was not supposed to be where I was. I didn't want to be found out, so I made up a name on the spot: "John Bergmann, one of the POWs at the castle—" I added nonchalantly and unsure. He did not seem surprised and said his name was Blackburn, and that he was or had been the game warden around here. We parted, and I slunk back through the bushes back home. I could have avoided that corner of the woods, but I wanted to explore it some more and ran into him again. "I asked at the Castle, but nobody knows a John Bergmann up there," he said and gave me a knowing smile. Whom had I tried to fool? He did not ask me my real name nor any other question and invited me to come with him to his house.

Somewhat uneasy I went along. Was there an official waiting for me? We came out of the trees and walked along a gently sloping wide meadow with a few gigantic oaks stretching their low branches close to the ground. He said, "That's where Indian soldiers had their camp a couple of years ago." Indian Soldiers? Of course, The British Empire!–I met Mrs. Blackburn, a kind middle-aged lady. And again they talked about those Indians who had cooked their meals there in the field right in front of the Blackburns' house. "And did they like their curry!" Curry? I had no idea what that was, but I did not ask. There I was sitting by a cosy fire with two friendly people who actually lived here, civilians, for the first time! What did I care about curry or for that matter the British Empire?

I came to see the Blackburns again and one day I was at Mr. Blackburn's house when a man, obviously a friend of theirs dropped in; his name was Ernie. He was short and stocky but not fat, and he was shy. As I learned from others, he had a slight paralysis when very young and had difficulty in closing one of his eyes. He worked in a slate quarry not far from Machen, and the dust and debris would often cause nasty infections in that eye. He always seemed to be self-conscious about his looks. Ernie was still working when I met him, but in his free time regularly came to the Blackburns on his motor bike to bring them whatever they needed, new batteries for their radio, things like that. He was the good spirit of the neighborhood, so I gathered, and also did errands for a Mr. Rees who lived down the hill, and Ernie thought I might want to meet him. But before that happened I met another "native."

April 9, 1946
Marvellous summer morning, but I cannot be glad of it. I'm still completely upset and confused from last night. If only Ilse were here. Horst, stay strong!

So what had happened that upset me so much? I had left the castle grounds as usual and had walked a bit farther down the slope and across the road and up again where they had been thinning trees, young larches. It was a glorious sunny day. The air was mild and sweet from the fresh sap that was oozing from the reddish cuts of the trunks and the broken branches all over in the luscious bright green of their young soft needles. I looked up to the pale blue sky, dreaming and happy. Two girls came cycling along the road and saw me up there in the clearing and stopped. Two girls, very young, teenagers, though one of them looked older. She was tall and slender and had pitch black hair. The dark red lipstick glowed in her pale face. She did all the talking. I don't remember who started the conversation and who said what. All I remember is the wonder and the excitement. I hadn't talked to a girl since I had left home two years ago. And the girls back home had been nothing like this. There had been more mature girls in our High School, and one or two of them even wore lipstick and went dancing. The older boys in my class talked about them, but I wasn't one of their set. The few girls I talked to did not wear lipstick, and none of them had such black hair. An exotic encounter–to me, and to the two Welsh teenagers? Perhaps they had been prowling around there just to catch a glimpse of those Germans. Surely the word about our arrival at Ruperra must have spread in the neighbourhood. And surely girls were told to stay away from us. What a temptation. All we did that afternoon was to look at each other and try to make conversation. Her name was Fiona. Fiona! What an unusual name. I had never heard or seen it. The other girl's name was Odette, and Fiona suggested that next time I bring a friend along for her.

I had to share my precious new secret, and asked Rudi–or was it Paul?–to come along. Whoever it was, he may not have liked his "blind date," he probably didn't like the whole idea and never came again. I think it was Paul who, a bit older than I, once had warned me not to get trapped. I might get into real trouble. "Once they get you into bed...."

I never saw Odette again. The next time Fiona came alone. We were sitting in the larch branches, I was leaning back, resting on my elbows. She was coming closer but not too close. I did not move. I remember that frozen position though inside I was all hot. She must have sensed my innocence, and was amused. We both laughed. She said something encouraging that to me sounded even boldly suggestive, but I did not, was not ready to take the hint. No, it did not turn into any kind of adolescent pulp. Nothing happened. No touching, nothing. But for days I couldn't think of anything else. And back among the other POWs, I had another secret to treasure. It was all so new and unexpected and wonderful. What a spring! At one of our "chance" meetings down by the larches she was singing: "I'll see you again, whenever spring comes through again, time may lie heavy between, but what has been is past forgetting." Some sentimental hit of the time. But all through the years since, that hit has held all the charm of that spring, all the expectation, the pungent fragrance of the larches and their vivid green of life.

April 13, 1946
Card to mother. Letter to Soltoft. Presently, I'm in the Chepstow camp for a week of dental treatment. Now I really notice the pressure of POW life behind barbed wire and realize the beauty of Ruperra Castle. I'm very glad to return next Friday. –Got a lovely letter

from Ilse yesterday, oh Ilse, how much is rushing in on me. Will you be able to understand me? Am I in a "good mood" right now! The camp life! The people, the barbed wire—

April 17, 1946
I am so glad we're back at the bakery. As I left Chepstow I got another letter from Ilse; I had just written her. In her letter I read the eagerness and the enthusiasm for university study. Yes, I too, am looking forward to it very much. Today for the first time I wrote her of my intention to study languages. What is she going to say—what is going on with Mother. I haven't heard from her for fourteen days. I also wrote Ilse about my experience as an "Englishman." I'm sure she'll understand me. I will not be disloyal to my own self.

April 19, 1946
My letters home must have been sometimes so "poetic," i.e., melancholy, that Mother felt the need to cheer me up. Even Russian soldiers could provide comic relief:

> I hope you can shoot the nuts again from the walnut tree when you want a strudel, but you'll have to get a new slingshot. The Russians confiscated it as a weapon. I miss it in your boy's corner, it was a souvenir of your childhood.
> Sleep well, my child. How happy I will be when you stretch out comfy in your bed.
>
> (March 13 1946)

And a handicraft flop could be as funny now as it had been years ago:

> I am making some gym shoes for Ilse. I hope they work better than the cycling shoes I made for you. [While I was riding downhill the soles disintegrated and got caught in the spokes.] Didn't we have some good times and laugh a lot in spite of all the things we had to do without? Now those merry days have become scarce but we shall find it again, the laughter that liberates. With all the nasty things nowadays, and when my good neighbours are "especially nice" to me, I remember that famous quote (from Goethe: "Kiss my arse!")

It was about time that I admitted happier moods in spite of my melodramatic guilt trip about Fiona.

Dear Mother!

At last mail from you of April 1. I am always so glad to read words in your letters that make me laugh. Then the sun shines twice as bright, and I can't help but enjoy the spring. I am often full of pep and do such crazy things that I fear the barbed wire has coiled around the wheels in my brain. Today I am going to do my washing so that I may qualify for resurrection. If only you could see me as a washerwoman!

April 21, 1946
Easter Sunday. Heavenly, sunny day. On Friday, at last a funny letter from Mother. Unforgettable ride to Machen and Trethomas. Exciting night by moonlight.

My most daring escapade on the borrowed bike. On and on, through the night, only the soft whirring of the tires on asphalt, on and on till I saw the red glow of the night shift at the pit in the small mining town. Why? I had not told Fiona, I had just taken off on a whim. Did I expect to meet her standing in the middle of the road in the moonlight waiting for me? The ride back and then the slow stretch up to the Castle. Quietly I leaned the bike back at its place in the doorway and crept back to bed. Everybody was asleep.

Easter, Monday, 1946
Somewhere I found this marker which reminded me of my grandfather, the forester, who had planted trees in the mountains south of Vienna.

THESE OAKS
RAISED FROM RUPERRA ACORNS
WERE PLANTED BY
THE HON. F.C. MORGAN M.P.

ON ST. DAVID'S DAY 1902

THE CORONATION YEAR OF
EDWARD VII.

JOHN MORGAN FORESTER
THOS. WATKINS WOODWARD

Fiona

Fiona in front of Ruperra Castle

Fiona

Ernie Oram

May 1, 1946
Since yesterday we have permission to walk within an area of a mile and a half in the vicinity of the castle. So we finally did achieve what we thought would be impossible. Now we don't have to slink around like criminals, so as not to be seen. Last night, together with Rudy, I followed bicycle tracks. Fiona. What an inexperienced, foolish boy I am! That's what I'm thinking now. With mail from home and the dear letters from Ilse, peace will return to me. But the impressions of the strange world which is opening before me so temptingly have to come to terms with the past and my future. Ilse's last letter included two spring flowers from home. How happy I was with this tenderness. And the very next day, I was looking down to the edge of the wood and walked the way again where I had met F. Horst, quo vadis? Oh, Mother knows me when she writes that my home country one day will be too small for me. Is it not the strange alluring sparkle in the large brown eyes that pulls me? Horst, stay strong. Ilse, too, had to fight like that and was victorious. Am I really after animal pleasures? Do I have to give in to them to realize how much I treasure Ilse?

May 2, 1946
Letter to Ilse. Now I feel a lot better since I told her as much as my letters allowed.

One day, a Sunday, I suppose, I walked up my hill of slender dark needle trees and down the other side, a discovery, an altogether different slope, a different mood: tall beeches with their bright green leaves, and vivid green grass and shrubs around the silvery gray trunks. And blue bells all over, blue as the sky way up between the branches of the beeches. Not a soul around. Where my trail joined another, wider one, I stopped. There, around an old beech, was an inscription carved into the bark in long lines:

> I SHALL PASS THROUGH THIS WORLD BUT ONCE.
> ANY GOOD THEREFORE THAT I CAN DO OR ANY KINDNESS
> THAT I CAN SHOW TO ANY HUMAN BEING,
> LET ME DO IT NOW.
> LET ME NOT DEFER OR NEGLECT IT
> FOR I SHALL NOT PASS THIS WAY AGAIN…

I could not believe what I saw. It must have taken hours to carve this. And who had done it? And how long ago? I ran my fingers over the letters; they were beginning to curl where the bark was growing back. I did not know the saying, familiarity did not blunt its meaning for me. I was moved–and puzzled. Only years later did I find out who had created this miracle in the woods.

Letters from Mother that reached me at this time:

> You need not worry about me. I have had training, and that's a lot, my treasure. I am grateful to my fate which never handled me with kid gloves. Of your things not much is missing. Only a dear human being or a loyal animal is irreplaceable. Don't be offended when I tell you that the life of all people strikes me as poorly played farce. (March 3, 1946)

> The sun has just gone down. It was a specially nice warm spring day. Ilse and I went picking stinging nettles for supper. You remember the soup. It's quite good. (April 1, 1946)

> Don't have a heavy heart, my son, because you can't be here yet with the others. Eat your bread with reverence. I hope you have enough of it. The time will come when we'll be together again. But a time may also come when your home country will be too small for you. We have green blood in our veins. I am old but distant lands pull me, too. If I only could come to you! (April 8, 1946)

May 3, 1946
Wrote to Mother: from the papers and other information I know how terrible the food situation at home must be even if you don't write about it. If I only could help.

A letter took at least three weeks in each direction. But the dates showed that we were much closer in thought.

On May 1 Mother had written:
> Greet the cedars from me. And use the time to eat your fill of bread. It is a rarity here.

On May 6 I wrote Mother:
> I hope the food situation is finally getting better. The newspapers are full of UNRRA help efforts but the shops are probably empty.

Mother was not worried about herself:

I have leased a small piece of ground, just for this year. Whether we will harvest or others who have not sown I can't tell. Last year a lot got stolen. Let's hope for the best. For my Sunday pleasure I weeded, and when I was done I thought now it should rain, and lo and behold it rained. Good! Good for the potatoes and the maize so that my son will have something to eat when he finally comes. You know, the achievement of the atom bomb and of bacteriological warfare I ungrudgingly leave to the great, but the achievement, to keep you my son from going hungry, that achievement I claim for myself alone. And that feeling will be as sublime for me as it is for the great to kill millions. I have to close now or I shall scream out into the whole world what moves my innermost being. But that concerns nobody but us two.

May 4, 1946

Yesterday I was supposed to go to Chepstow for health reasons. But I succeeded in staying behind since I have no intention of being transferred to a different work camp, and I hardly believe I am sick enough to be repatriated.

May 10, 1946

I am happy. There are two beautiful letters from Ilse. Most of all, I am happy about her suggestion that I should study languages, and in the last letter I had written exactly that! Ilse, how much your letters help me. They give me strength again! I've just finished, with Paul, the biology questions for Fiona. Tomorrow I shall hand them to her. At the end I wrote "The last sunbeams are falling through the leaves of the chestnut trees and are painting golden stains on the moss. And there in the middle of the moss, a small never-before-seen foreign looking flower is dreaming. Its dishevelled head is directed to the setting sun, as if to look behind the veils of an unknown world. Cool dusk is falling on the earth. But suddenly, a strange warm wind breathes across the grass—it is coming from that distant world the small flower is so curious to turn to....How lovely and soft is this breath—how tenderly it is playing around that little bloom, alluring, persuading, and singing such a sweet tune "Come with me, come with me..." and the flower listens and listens....

But the roots are too strong, and the wind is too weak—for the roots come from the opposite side of the brook. The night is singing deeper and darkening and the wind goes on breathing and playing until it will find a new flower.

Whether she understands it? If not, I can't do anything about it. It wasn't worth the while. And if she does, will she come again? In another part of the letter, I wrote: "and use the human mind to perform immoderate transgressions in the satisfaction of their instincts. Consequently, man is no longer master of himself but is commanded by the beast in himself. He has sunk from the highest top of creation into the gutter."

One would think that Fiona and I had been engulfed in the wildest, most reckless abandonment—when there was really nothing going on. I don't remember what orgies my wishful thinking conjured up. My imagination didn't have too much to work with. I often did not know what the soldiers were talking about when they were on topic number one, and exchanged memories and tricks about how to arouse a woman. The very fact that I could be attracted to another girl started a torrent of guilt feelings that must have had their own attraction, or I wouldn't have wallowed in them with such false pathos. Fiona was not in the mood for any kind of soul-searching. She was getting ready for her botany exam, and had asked me to put together some study questions for her. I did not feel competent and asked Paul, the forester, and he, good friend, obliged. She answered the questions and added a few personal lines; she cut right through the mush in my florid letter referring to my blatant symbolism as the "ecology question" and added "am I the flower or the breeze? If the breeze, the roots may be on the other side of the water but a typhoon can force a ship three miles inland. So I feel sorry for such feeble roots with such a force." and in spite offending her letter with "But what has been is past forgetting," her realism was undiminished: "I did not think you were writing as a lover who could not live without me; anybody who does that is mad. But you wrote because you wanted something, as usual. I am very handy I admit and God never put breath into a greater fool than I. I cannot get the book you want, and I don't intend going to a library for it." (It was probably a book of English literature).

And the other letter I kept:

> Today I had your letter. Since you wrote in English; I write in German [faulty but perfectly understandable German]. I am concerned that I get caught when I am with you. It is better not to come so often, but when I don't come you say that I am with the English boys. You forget that I am English and that you love a German girl.
>
> I know that the grammar in this letter is atrocious. I know that you will excuse that. I could write many words in English but it is dangerous.

> I had to come because when I don't come you do such fragile [sic] things. For example you write letters to me, come to Trethomas etc.
>
> Yours ever, F.

I don't remember ever having gone to Trethomas after that memorable bike ride when I had not ventured into the town but turned when I came too close. But apparently I had done not only that but also "etc." Two years later she wrote to me back in Vienna: "Why do you wish that I had forgotten that letter you pushed through the door? My mother kept it." The letter that I had wisely hoped she would forget must have been that melodramatic "ecological" one. And her mother even kept it! Maybe she was more romantic than her daughter.

May 14, 1946
Since yesterday we know that the bakery will be closed on the 31st of May. Now we have to make the best of the last few days. (The following I must have considered top secret because I wrote part of it in German shorthand!). *Ernie holds rather communist views.* (Actually he was an ILP man). Yesterday he took me to his mother who lives with him on the other side of my lookout hill. I knew that Ernie's father had been killed in an air-raid on Coventry, but his mother was as friendly to me as Ernie always had been. Their cottage was very homely. Ernie had some German records; he cranked up the gramophone and we listened to Marlene Dietrich. A warm, cosy evening in a Welsh cottage. I especially remember the huge hunk of meat in cheese cloth hanging from the low ceiling above the blazing fire. Much later Ernie told me that his mother said: "You'll never see anything on that wall better than that!"

May 19, 1946
Met Fiona. She gave me the answers to the biology questions, and ended her note with: "I'll see you again whenever Spring comes through again–time may lie heavy between, but what has been is past forgetting." In spite of it all, I've regained my balance and am glad about it. Today I started my notebook on English literary history.

The Fiona adventure ended a few days later:

I finally broke with her completely, and this morning the sky was twice as clear. Most of all, I'm looking forward to Ilse's next letter which I can read unperturbed. I am so glad that

I still have a will in me, although it wasn't all that hard to say no to her. However, if the occasion had presented itself I would certainly not have stopped at this point [Will or no Will?] *As it is, I draw the final conclusion: The liking of adventure drew us together, the different opinion of love separated us.*

Fiona had given me a passport photo of herself. Much later I wrote on the back of it:

> And I am glad, yea, glad with all my heart,
> That thus so cleanly I myself can free.

I had found the lines in Palgrave's and thought they were the perfect epitaph for the Fiona-episode. Now I really could forget it. It slowly emerged again out of oblivion in 1990. Alun Lewis's *Collected Stories* had just been published. In the story "The Poetry Class" a teacher reads Drayton's poem. The two lines flashed in my memory, but it took me some time to connect them with a person. Only the photograph brought Fiona back. I read the story again with the "half-shameful attention" of the students in the story, realizing how little our episode justified connecting it with the poem. But in 1946? In adolescence all feelings are poetry.

I still have to overcome a sentimental weakness but I get help in that from Rees, Blackburn, Greenmeadow.

That help had started while I was still seeing Fiona.

May 19, 1946

When I was at Blackburns' the day before yesterday, Ernie took me to Mr. Rees, an old bachelor who lives with his sister and pursues his hobbies. I believe he is the right man for me. He has an amazing knowledge of history and lives in a charming, enchanted old house. I shall visit him again tomorrow.

May 21, 1946

Yesterday at Rees's again. I copied poems from his books. I always come home loaded with books. Today I started a notebook on English literature.

Of all the cautious entries in my journal this was the most hedging even if it was only meant to hint at anther secret event, but it shows my hope to meet an "interesting" person. It was true, Ernie did not have all that much time, and shy as he was, did not talk much. From the day I was first at Greenmeadow I lived on four levels. To my "adventure" with Fiona there was now added that at Greenmeadow. Neither knew of the other, but both pushed my "official" existence at the bakery completely into the background. Fairly soon Fiona, too, faded, and during my last few weeks in Wales

Greenmeadow was more on my mind than anything else. While all this was going on in me and around me, letters from home and my, as we thought, imminent repatriation surrounded everything else with a special ambivalence. The present was all the more intense because it would not last, and would become memory once I was home again. In what follows, the different levels will intermingle. Much as the journal may reflect all that Fiona meant to me, it says very little about Greenmeadow, and it was that experience which engraved itself most vividly and most lastingly in my memory.

Ernie thought I would enjoy meeting Mr. Rees. I suspect he was so unassuming that he thought Mr. Rees would offer me more than he could. I was curious and glad to meet any civilian, so Ernie took me along. He left his cycle at the Blackburns', and we walked down the slope with the old gnarled oaks and over the brook and up a little to Greenmeadow, the house where Mr. Rees lived.

From the very first moment Mr. Rees was extremely friendly. The fact that I was a German POW made no difference to him; for me it made his hospitality all the more precious. I was made welcome and invited to come again, as often as I felt like it, and at my second visit Mr. Rees asked me to sign his guest book. After my silly masquerade with Blackburn I probably was uneasy a moment, afraid that he might want to check my identity. I don't remember which name I signed. But even if I kept up my Bergmann-lie–and he must have found out about it sooner or later–the Reeses never asked any questions, either out of respect for the privacy of others, even a POW, or out of tact. They would not have wanted to embarrass me. I was their guest. Ernie probably had introduced me simply as "John, one of the German boys at the castle," and John was my name at Greenmeadow forever after.

What did I call them? Mr. and Miss Rees? I don't remember ever addressing them so formally; it did not seem necessary to address them by name at all. It all happened so naturally. Mr. Rees was an old gentleman, to me he looked ancient, but he was probably not much older than I am now, seventy-five. He was thin and bony, and spoke with an old man's voice, slow but not shaky, clear and precise, an educated voice. His mind was crystal clear. He never talked about his life, a career he might have had. He seemed to be beyond all that, a gentleman of leisure. I never learned how he had come to live at Greenmeadow, and had the impression that he had lived there with his hardly younger sister Mary a very long time, if not all of their lives.

Mr. Rees would show me everything around and inside the house with an unobtrusive pride: the luxurious clematis that was climbing all over the bower trellises close to the garden gate, an old tree he was especially fond of with a gnarled trunk and branches going in all directions, a miraculous laburnum full of tresses of purple, yellow, and white blossoms, a rarity, as Mr. Rees emphatically pointed out to me. There was also a rowan tree, apple and pear trees, gooseberry bushes and a bed with kitchen greens. The garden was not neglected but showed no signs of obtrusive interference, the grass grew tall between the trees, and everything was all the more beautiful because it grew in the freedom of early summer when nothing is trimmed or cut.

From the sunshine, fragrance, and color we walked into the dark, cool house and into history. My friendly guide drew my attention to the flagstones in the hall; some markings and the way they were laid out indicated to him that the house had at one time been a chapel. The stones certainly were worn unevenly enough. And in the National Museum of Wales in Cardiff there was some ancient relic that Rees had found around the house. There was an atmosphere about the house, change had never touched it.

I am not sure why the Reeses took me to their hearts. Neither of them had ever been to Europe, and perhaps I was as exotic to them as they were to me. I doubt that they had ever seen or talked to a foreigner or had one at their house, let alone a German POW. They might have wondered what one of those boys at the castle was like, but there was no intrusive curiosity about them; they just took me in and soon I felt like a family member dropping by. I didn't go to Greenmeadow every evening but often enough to feel at home there. I was not alone as I often was at the camps where so many people were around me and talked about the same thing, the home far away. I usually stayed the evening, and the evenings were long. It was June. There was no need to ever turn the light on while I was there. Did they have electricity at Greenmeadow? I know that there was no radio, and it was hard to imagine that anything as harsh and sudden as a switch could ever break the soft twilight mood. I might have stayed too long at times, but my generous hosts would never let me know it. The time would come for me to walk up the hill back to the castle. Sometimes the tall grass down by tile brook would be still wet from a shower or damp from the evening air, and Mr. Rees never failed to warn me to keep my feet dry at all times; he would wrap heavy brown paper round my feet and tie it with string around my ankles, he was so concerned. And when I turned back before I would be out of sight, the two would wave from the little garden gate sagging on the hinges. My buddies at camp got used to my absence and covered for me; one evening the Sergeant Major screamed: "Where is that Jarka?" and they screamed back, " in the bath tub."

And that was that. He probably just left disgusted. But I never heard about it in the morning.

I had supper up at the camp, but I would not stuff myself whenever I was going to see the Reeses that evening. I knew they were going to offer me a little something during the evening, and I could not refuse and disappoint them. I was always asked to sit in the chair of honor, an armchair in front of the fireplace. There always was a kettle on the hob over the coal fire, and Mr. Rees would hand me the long-handled toasting fork, and I would get closer to the fire, and hold a slice or two against the coals which glowed in the evening light. The clock in the already dark hall would rattle and finally strike the hour. The toast was done, and Miss Rees would come from the kitchen with tea and butter and honey or jam, and on special occasions a gooseberry tart! What I treasure especially about those meals was the question of the egg. The lady of the house wanted to know what kind of egg she should soft boil for me, "Hen or goose?"–very soon a purely rhetorical question, because Mr. Rees would give me his well-meaning smile and say: "Take the goose egg, John; it's bigger." He was sure that I was hungry, and I wasn't, but in Greenmeadow everything tasted better because of the atmosphere there, the hominess and the kindness with which it was offered. And while I was munching my simple home-made delicacies, Mr. Rees would talk to me or read me some odd bit of news or a joke or anecdote. And then Miss Rees would clean up and, through the door, I could see two cups upside down on their saucers on the kitchen table, ready for breakfast. I don't remember that they ever ate anything while I was there. It was almost hard to imagine them eating anything. They didn't seem to need it.

Miss Rees usually left the talking to us and shuffled back and forth between kitchen and hearth. It seems that she would only break her silence to tell me, not necessarily before my repast, not in any serious tone but with the humour of an often repeated nursery rhyme (I probably should have chimed in as a child would have):

> Come to your places
> With clean hands and faces
> And pay good attention to all you are told.
> Or else you will never
> Be handsome or clever
> For talking is silver
> But silence is gold.

To me, Miss Rees' cautionary verse was her theme song, and I copied it into my special note book to memorize, the latest lines I had picked up in my evening school from my gentle teachers. And later my children heard it often when we sat down to eat even if none of us followed any of the admonitions. But everybody knew where they came from.

Aunt Mary not only followed what she "preached," she was also a little cautious in other things. One afternoon two men had been announced to shear the two sheep in the back of the house. But it was not clear whether they would come while I was there. And here they were all of a sudden. Miss Rees pushed me, no she would never do that, she gently but firmly told me to step into the back room next to the kitchen, "will you please," so that the sheep shearers would not see me. Who knows what they might think or, heaven forbid, say to others—a foreigner at Greenmeadow? Possibly a runaway German from the castle having tea? So I slipped away into hiding. But was it the right room? From the window I could just catch a glimpse of the two bending over the sheep. I stepped back into a safe corner. I wonder whether Mr. Rees was that careful, and would not have preferred to defend his right to have a guest, any guest.

My hours at Greenmeadow held a gentle excitement for me. Mr. Rees loved to show me things, and though I have forgotten many particulars, I do remember the politeness that accompanied even the slightest and shortest transaction. I would thank him for handing me the newspaper clipping, letter or poem, read it and hand it back to him saying, "Thank you!" And with a slight nod Mr. Rees would say, "Thank you, John!" completing the little ceremony which was so characteristic of his natural thoughtfulness. I was not used to such courtesy back home, and the army and POW camps were hardly the places to learn it. I took it as the mark of a true English gentleman. When we went to another room or out into the garden, Mr. Rees invariably insisted that I go ahead. When I would not hear of it, he at last took the lead but not without saying: "The dust before the broom," but when the game went on too long and I was the one to give in and go ahead, he would say: "The dog following his master." I just could not win. Of course, this ritual of polite self-deprecation was always observed with a smile and a twinkle in his eyes.

One time I followed him or he followed me up some creaky stairs to a fairly large parlour-like room, that wasn't used very much anymore. There was a heavy dresser or bookcase in that room with a row of large red-backed leather volumes and a sort of portrait gallery all along the walls, photographs of people Mr. Rees had known. The wide floorboards would sag a little as

Mary Rees ("Aunt Mary") and William J. B. Rees ("Uncle William")

Greenmeadow

we walked from one to the next and stopped at each. Rees would look at the faces and tell me their names and what their station in life had been and what happened to them. Every introduction would end with Uncle William's soft and melancholy "Well, well, he's been gone for...thirty or forty years now." All these ghosts looked very respectable in their stiff Sunday best pose; a spot of mildew here and there only added to their dignity as they stared at me from their dusty frames. Only one of these old friends on the wall was still alive, and Mr. Rees chuckled as he told me that this man was a real character. It was nothing extraordinary in his behaviour, it was just that he had always pronounced mischievous on the second syllable and added the "i"after the "v"on purpose–this "Mr. Mischeevious" as Rees would call him. This name came up again and again in our conversations, just for the fun of it. Mr. Rees had a gentle, whimsical sense of humour, and he liked puns; the one I remember was about a ewe under a yew tree; he wrote it out for me on a piece of paper.

Mr. Rees's handwriting was unique, not because it was just old-fashioned. He did not use one of those nibs that produce elegant hair and shadow lines. He wrote with a quill! I had never seen anybody write with a quill except in an old painting perhaps or in a movie about some event in history. As I was watching Mr. Rees moving the quill fairly fast over the paper I thought I was back two hundred years. Change had not reached Greenmeadow; that was the charm of the place, and for me the quill symbolized that timelessness more than anything else. My wonder delighted Mr. Rees, and, with visible pleasure, he demonstrated to me how this venerable skill was practiced. He did not use the whole feather but only the bottom part, and he had a penknife in the original sense of the word: an instrument to cut the quill and make the little slit in its tip. He never wrote with anything but quills. Where did he get them? In 1946!? I had heard and seen the two geese behind the house; obviously they were there not just for their large eggs as I had assumed.

Once I asked him to write a verse in my notebook; he did so from memory. It was in spirit very much like many others he recited:

> When I am old I shall not care
> > To deck with flowers my faded hair.
> 'Twill be no vain desire of mine
> > In rich and costly dress to shine,
> Bright jewels and the brightest gold
> > Will charm me not when I am old.

Oh yes, the roof! When I came one evening, Mr. Rees greeted me from the roof. The tiles often demanded attention and his age did not keep him away from them. There he was at the top of a long ladder working away, and the cat was sitting beside him. "Dinky watches everything I do," he said as he carefully came down rung after rung. I could get a close look at his shoes then, sturdy walking shoes. He showed me his heavy cast iron cobbler's last on which he kept his foot wear in good order to keep his feet dry all year. He put new soles on, it seemed as many of them as the shoe would take, and pounded round-headed nails all over soles and heels. These shoes were made to last, and there was an almost medieval look about them that went well with the house and the quill. Ernie, on his motorcycle, kept Mr. Rees supplied with leather and nails and shoe grease and anything else that was needed, and he would not forget "kippers for the cat," the cat that supervised the repairs of roof and shoes. There was one claim of everyday reality that Mr. Rees could not handle himself: the coal. The lorry dumped it at the side of the road and, from there, it had to be transported down the hill, over the little bridge and up to the house. I suppose usually Ernie would take care of that, but when Mr. Rees spoke of this recurring dilemma, I offered to help and persuaded Paul to come along. He was the only one of the camp crew who knew of Fiona and could be safely trusted with some contact with my latest discovery. Besides that he was a muscular forester and could load the wheelbarrow much heavier than I could. The job was done in a few trips, and Mr. Rees was so very grateful. He never forgot our rescue mission, as he called it.

This old man who seemed to live in a different age could very well take care of reality whenever it invaded the idyllic remoteness of Greenmeadow, and not only the old realities of roofs and shoes. He was not only and not always a dreamer; he had a quiet dignity about him, and his gentleness was not not weakness. He could be a fighter. He would never talk about it, and I had to learn from others that, as a councilor, he had taken on the Bishop over some trust fund that was to benefit the poor of the parish and had been mismanaged or worse. As Ernie put it: "There was that charity problem. Mr. Rees never got to the bottom of it. They wanted him to sign a report that everything was fine. He said: "His Honour the Bishop's signature will be on it? But W. J. B. Rees's signature will not be on it."

It may have been this sense of justice that made him so sympathetic with us prisoners of war who were held so long after the end of hostilities. I was probably the first prisoner he had ever met face-to-face, and my twenty years may have confirmed his pity as the word "prisoner" stirred his imagination with a surprising twist as touching as it was naive. "Do you live in the dungeon, John?" he asked me one evening and in his voice was real concern. I must have looked at him in amazement. He was serious. How could that be? This was 1946! I knew he was sincere, and I was so amazed that the question did not strike me as funny at all; so I reassured him that we did not live in damp darkness but as normally as any British soldier in Nissen huts. Fortunately it did not occur to me to tell him that the only creature that had lived in the Ruperra Castle dungeon in recent times had been a young pig that even regained its freedom. That would have broken the spell. His imagination returned to the images that the word "prisoner" had evoked, and one evening as we sat in the twilight he opened a big heavy book with a thick red leather spine, and started reading:

> My hair is grey, but not with years,
>   Nor grew it white
>   In a single night
> As men's have grown from sudden fears.
> My limbs are bowed, though not with toil...

and as I listened to stanza after stanza in the soft voice of the old man in front of me in the dusk, I listened to the prisoner himself telling me his life's tragedy.

Was it poetry then that had made Mr. Rees ask me that puzzling question? He was always quoting some lines of poetry, mostly melancholy reflections on human nature and the human condition, the vanity of human wishes, the passing of beauty and pain – "Even this shall pass away," he often reminded me. And some of the verses and sayings he would copy with his quill for me to keep. He was of a different age and, to me, he personified a life away from the war, away from the brutality and ugliness I had witnessed in Europe and in the other camps. When I record his anachronistic "quaintness," which may appear ludicrous or pathetic, I do so not only in affectionate recollection. In Mr. Rees I was in the presence of an imagination that was as childlike and pure and naive as poetry itself.

It was soon after I had come to Greenmeadow that a significant shift in my literary pastime occurred.

In Ruperra there were no cultural programs, no more lectures on *Faust*, but that work was never out of my mind. Ilse wrote about two productions she had recently seen in Vienna, and in almost every letter she quoted a

Uncle William

When I am old I shall not care
To deck with flowers my faded hair,
'Twill be no vain desire of mine
In rich and costly dress to shine,
Bright jewels and the brightest gold
Will charm me naught when I am old

passage. I had continued reading and copying German poems by hand, and on the typewriter. I had pieced together a little history of German literature, had attempted to write verse in my own language. I had made a little book of all of this and bound it in the finer, more densely woven material of heavy-weight flour bags of a beige hue, my special bakery buckram. And I glued in two illustrations which I had treasured from previous camps: the one was very much in tune with all that German poetry: the lovely smiling face of Reglindis from Naumburg Cathedral that my fatherly companion in the Sheffield sick ward had given me. The other was L'Inconnue de la Seine which I had ripped out of a cheap magazine from a trash can. Her mysterious smile appealed to my vague romanticism that considered her the perfect "frontispiece" for Rilke's *Cornet*.

But all along with my German literary selections I had been reading English. I had found an anthology of German and English lyrics, and was so taken with the music of Swinburne's "I hid my heart in a nest of roses" that I remember to this day the last stanza. But more than by the "secret bird" of Swinburne's "Dreamland" I was lured by the language around me, and I used every chance to speak it. The closer I came to English-speaking people the more I became obsessed with learning the language of the country that the war had landed me in, and often I welcomed that transplantation with a blasphemous egotism, as if the war had had no other purpose than to give me a chance to learn English. The attitude that I held then in my inquisitive youth makes me think of Fritz Kalmar's short story "Good luck in bad luck," in which a Viennese talks about the first World War: "The Italians had declared war on Austria. What a catastrophe!" But for me? A stroke of luck, I came to the Italian front, ...the sunrise from a trench in the mountains, what a glorious sight! And then 1918, the collapse of the Monarchy. What a tragedy!! But for me another stroke of luck. They took me prisoner and sent me to a camp in Naples. I had never thought I would see the sea, and there it was. Magnificent!" And I, having grown up poor in a small town on the Danube and having sent my dreams with the freighters that chugged up and down the river, their foreign flags waving from their stern, had never thought I would ever see the world, and here I was in faraway Wales!

I had continued living my emotional life in German, writing my journal, writing and receiving letters from home. But the living contact with English-speaking people, with the soldiers, with Fiona, Ernie and above all with Mr. Rees and his sister, opened English as a living alternative to German. No matter how moralistic or didactic or Romantic the poems were that Mr. Rees read to me, they were poetry read aloud by a "native," and not just read by myself, stumbling through lines. As I had done in German, I now began compiling myself a sort of basic history of English literature with much better sources than I had had for German, the books I lugged up to the castle: for example *British Bards or Choice Selections from the Works of the Principal Poets of England from Spenser to Cowper,* Norwich, printed by and for John Stacy and sold in London 1820. From it I copied Shakespeare's Sonnets, poems by Wither, Milton, Parnell, Gray's "Elegy," Pope's "Ode to Solitude" and on and on to Cowper's "Task." Another book was from the set with the heavy red leather spine in Mr. Rees's upstairs picture gallery: *The Poets Library* volume VI, Arranged and Compiled by Arthur Stockwell, London, Arthur Stockwell Ltd., 29 Ludgate Hill, and from it I copied Byron's "Prisoner of Chillon," of course, and his "When we two parted" and others. All of that made up hefty notebook pages which I held together with heavier black paper I had discovered in my store room; I bound them with the strong staples from the discharged flour sacks. Flour paste was the perfect glue to spread the coarse brown jute from those sacks over the large folder complete with side flaps which I had made to hold my treasures together in one floppy "clothbound volume."

I doubt that much of all that poetry actually sank in as I copied it in a neat hand. A teacher more concerned with form than knowledge would have commended my labors for their exemplary diligence. I must have gained some feel for poetic diction. But Parnell's "Hermit," Goldsmith's "Traveller," Shakespeare's "Passionate Pilgrim, " all the "thou's" and "ere's," the classical allusions and metric elisions did not prepare me for reading twentieth-century newspapers any more than did Mr. Rees's quotations which called for the quill and would have resisted a typewriter.

And yet Greenmeadow was not completely immune to the present. After all, Mr. Rees was a Councillor, regularly attended meetings in Cardiff, and must have heard people talk about what was in the papers even if he did not read them himself; I don't remember ever seeing a recent newspaper at Greenmeadow. But his one question about recent German history sounded as unreal to me as his question about whether we lived in the Ruperra dungeon: "John is it true, that the SS ate babies?" I did not write this question in my journal. Sometimes memory is more reliable. That was not a question to be forgotten easily. But to me it sounded like a bit of English scare propaganda against the Huns of World War I. In Chepstow I had seen the pictures of Bergen Belsen and later I knew that his question about Nazi bestiality wasn't at all as anachronistic and outrageous as it sounded to me then. I had not believed what the films had documented, and I don't remember my answer, but I probably denied that there could possibly be any substance to what he was asking about. There was one soldier in our group who wore a uniform jacket of the Waffen-SS, whether his own or not, I don't know. He was our expert confectioner who made all those layer cakes for the officers and the delicious pastry for us. And he should have killed children, or even eaten them? Ridiculous. I did not know Hannah Arendt's *The Banality of Evil* or I would have connected pastry with murder which I hope would have been completely unfair to our cook. He did not at all look like those SS-men at that bridge who were ready to kill German soldiers on retreat. I just could not imagine him exchanging his cooking spoon for a pistol.

Mr. Rees's question that evening could have opened a discussion about the Holocaust. But we never talked about that in Greenmeadow. The peace there was never broken by unpleasant truths. I have often wondered about that since. My time at Ruperra delayed my political awareness, my willingness to see through the denial and the psychological repression that must have been so general in POW-camps—among soldiers who only wanted to get home. But perhaps the unquestioning kindness I found at Green-meadow, in Mr. and Miss Rees, and Ernie helped to reaffirm values on which such an awareness had to be based. Greenmeadow in its timelessness was for me a refuge from history, but it also led me back to the timelessness of human warmth beyond national and linguistic boundaries, and how could I ever forget Ernie who had lost his father in a bombing raid on Coventry and treated me, the German soldier, like a younger brother.

My ties to Greenmeadow were to become even closer. One weekend the Reeses' niece had come from Newport on one of her regular visits. She was not married and about forty years old as I guessed from Mr. Rees's remarks at some later time. She looked very Welsh to me with her round head and dark hair, with some grey in it, and her lively dark brown eyes. And she was lively in her talk and her gestures. She had been to Germany as a student in the Thirties, spoke no German but had climbed the Watzmann mountain in Bavaria and, when after Dunkirk the invasion had threatened, she had gotten her mountain boots ready to take to the Welsh hills. She was most interested in my POW story, in Austria, my family, and my study plans.

Mr. Rees must have shown me a letter with her name on it: Jones, Vivian, B.A., and that's why in my Journal I gave her my secret code name: JONBA. She was an elementary school teacher, and she always talked about correcting themes, so I assume she taught English. She certainly was most interested in my attempts to improve my English as only a teacher dedicated to the mother tongue could be. She could only come out to Greenmeadow on weekends, but I remember her presence there as vividly as if there had been many more Saturdays than were actually left before I had to leave Ruperra and Greenmeadow.

What did we talk about? What did we not talk about? Books and school and her brothers and my folks at home and when I would be back there. And one day she brought along her nephew Roger, a lively three or four-year old. He would climb up on my knees, and with shouts of delight, uncurl my closed fist finger by finger to see what I was holding in it. With children you don't need language to communicate. But how much did speaking English influence the way I came across to others; did changing languages change me? My uncertainty must have come up again and again. Much later, Viv wrote in a letter:

> I realise what a barrier language can be. Had you not known English, I would never have known you. But your knowing English alone could never have provided us with our friendship. I am convinced of that. Until I was seven I could speak nothing but Welsh, my home language dominated. Then gradually, because the school language, English, became all important and all my friends spoke English, Welsh faded, and I thought and spoke in English. But I do not think you feel in a language. I think feelings are universal and pass easily from one person to another. I am quite sure my feelings are the same whether I speak in English or in Welsh. And that I am the same individual entity. I have not acquired an additional personality.
>
> It is impossible to be a different person than the one you really are. Speaking another language should not make you feel that you are living another being. If you are sincere you can only be your true self whatever language you speak.
>
> I have no sense that you are a foreigner. A difference in language makes no difference to me. In fact I have met many, many English speaking people whose ideas, ways of thought and feelings are quite foreign to me. What do you think?

I don't remember how I answered that question.

May 28, 1946
Yesterday and today and this morning, nasty rain. And now the sun is beaming again. How clear and pure the air is. The wind sweeps above the hills and drives the white clouds on and on. And down there, how beautifully smooth and silvery the sea. How fond I've gotten of this view! The alluring water between the treetops and the rich green of the cedars and cypresses in the foreground, the rhododendrons in their gorgeous red and violet! And there the magpies are flying and I must sit here and cannot fly out with them, not even on the bicycle, into all this glory. How would I race them down to the Channel, down to the bank, down to the shore that beckons me. And on and on, out there without end. But the sun is shining so beautifully I cannot be sad.

May 31, 1946
Today we delivered by truck what is left of the yeast, etc., to Hereford via Pontypool, Abergavenny. Have lunch at Hereford. Torrent of rain. Drive back in better weather. Near Abergavenny, we can make out the Sugar Loaf and the other high mountains in the vicinity. We take awfully wet and stinking empty flour sacks to the harbor in Cardiff, at first to Spiller's, a big mill on the quay with ships right next to it. Then after a long odyssey through the dark quarters with Negroes and Mulattos, we finally get rid of the mess at Rand's. Now the sun is shining again and we leave Cardiff at top speed. On the beautifully smooth Bristol Channel two large ships…Unfortunately, the canteen couldn't take my letters to Ilse because I had forgotten to put them in the mailbox. Beautiful evening. I grab the bike. Douglas Firs, St. Melons, Cefn Mably. Rees unfortunately in bed already. Now I'm really wiped out. Yesterday our work here in the bakery came to its end, and I must surrender to my fate.

June 7, 1946
A beautiful day comes to its end. Again. I just read Ilse's letter again, and Mother, too, had written. And even from Walter Wolfgang, I got an English letter. He wrote me about all the other classmates.

Klosterneuburg 17.V. 1946

Dear Horst!
For you have written in English, I'll answer in the same language. This is the second letter I wrote you. The first one was lost by the boy who was to post it. I hope you'll not be too angry that I answer so lately. As to our school comrades

I shall count down as we sat in the classroom. Moenia is back from captivity and studying. He is always the old one. Our Zwick died in the last days of the war in Rhineland. I am so sorry. His parents got the obituary last March, I myself am happily engaged and study German and English languages. "Uncle" Müller is still a railway official and studying law on the side. Schlicky sent a letter from Russia before a few weeks. Stifter is still a prisoner but I don't know where he is. Otto is a prisoner in Russia and is working in a factory. Posenbauer is attending night school. Of Watschelgans I know nothing. His mother was killed before a few days by burglars as we read in the newspaper. Schilcher is back from captivity and now living in Upper Austria. Bona studies geography, Stradner is engaged with his Ilse Forster and studies law and keeps back from us. Karpf lives in Salzburg and has a job as an interpreter with the Americans. Justi, the old philosopher, studies German and History. I am so sorry to say we buried Parak Venerand before 14 days. He died of the shot in his lungs. We brought him the last regards by our class. Engelberger studies biology. Wohlmut attends the college of agricultures. Kienzel is studying chemistry. Rudi Schatz fell in 1944 in Italy. Kutuso is in captivity in Russia. Aigner became papa and husband, I don't know what he became first. Papa I am afraid. Karasek crashed down at Prague and got killed. That is about all of our old Octava. And with regard to the study conditions: few books, few professors, many pupils and holidays. But everything else is ok. I think you know all that I can report you. Come and see more. That will do for today. I hope to hear more of you and your life so far from home. The best is, you personally come and tell me.

With best regards,
Yours sincerely,
Wolfi

I had not been very close to most of the boys he mentioned, and scribbled my not very emotional comment on the back of the letter – in English:

Vivian Jones ("Viv")

Page from Horst Jarka's Journal

> Some go east, and some go west
> Some north, some south and some to rest.

My journal entry was equally cold:

"Once more you near me, wavering apparitions." (Faust) The war drove us ahead on life's path on into a time when day after day one of us disappears...

I spent the evening so pleasantly with Rees. The night air is beautifully warm. Yes, the Linden trees will be in bloom again. The second time without me. It's so beautifully still.

> *"O'er all the hilltops is quiet now*
> *In all the treetops hearest thou*
> *Hardly a breath.*
>
> *The birds are asleep in the trees*
> *Wait, soon like these*
> *Thou, too, shall rest..." (Goethe, translated by Tennyson)*

June 12, 1946

Back from Rees. Also from Blackburn. Oh, this exquisite peace! Yesterday I got a German-English dictionary from Jonba and I'm so grateful for it. Perhaps that was the last time that I will see her. There is something really magnificent about friendship. I'm already feeling the loss. I'm not sure but is it the strange circumstances that made me feel that good-bye so deeply. Eternal idealism.

June 16, 1946

Saw Jonba again. She gave me the Penicillin brochure. What would mother say? I must write more.

The penicillin story reminded me of Mother. She had volunteered to be a nurse in a field hospital on the Italian Front 1915-1918, and was a prisoner of war afterwards. She had often told me that whenever mould formed on a soldier's gangrened wound he was saved. There was something in that mould that healed it.

June 19, 1946

Just finished an English paper. This kind of study is excellent. As if she didn't have enough papers to correct for school, Viv was eager to correct the English in my translations from the German on a mixed bag of topics depending on what short German texts I could find in the German language POW newspaper. I still have some with her pencilled corrections: "The Spirit of English Sports," "Harold Laski," "An English Faust in the Age of Shakespeare," "The Times of Day. Runge's Painting," "Sir Oliver Wren," etc., etc. And on one of our last Saturdays she brought me two gifts that proved very precious to me: Palgrave's poetry anthology *The Golden Treasury*, and the Pelican edition of a *Short History of English Literature* by B. Ifor Evans!

Mother wrote: "I am pleased that you are so serious about your learning English. Mastering the language will surely be useful to you here, and you will learn to know and respect the people who speak it when you penetrate their character and special qualities." And she appreciated the friendliness I had received as a POW.

In my mail home I never mentioned Greenmeadow because I did not want to cause my friends there any inconvenience from the authorities. But from my general remarks, Mother could tell that I had nothing to complain about. Had she known details, she would have found many more words for her appreciation.

> I am very happy to know that you like the country there so much. I am sure that there, too, are good people. (May 22 1946)
>
> Can you imagine how happy I am that you are well and how grateful I am to the country that I have never seen and that makes my son's life so tolerable! (June 23 1946)

Finally I concocted a family-friend from before the war who lived in England to prepare Mother for mail from Viv, and indirectly suggested my classmate Wolfi as an interpreter. I initiated this contact before mail would become unpredictable once I had left Ruperra. That day was coming nearer.

June 24, 1946

Viv had arrived and suggested a hike. Mr. Rees lent me his salt and pepper pants, and some shirt or jacket. Clothes make the man, especially a POW incognito.

Yesterday we spent a beautiful Sunday afternoon. The morning mist had risen, and although it was still sultry, it was magnificent. We walked up from Greenmeadow through the woods to the road and up a steep wooded path to the ridge. At the highest point the ordinance survey marker said: Craig Llysfaen 869ft. At our feet Cardiff, in the mist and the smoke, and way back there, some white spots. Must be the Civic Center. Yes, now I can see the towers of City Hall. The bed of the Channel is covered with a layer of leaden haze, hiding the shore beyond, and yet it seems to be a leaden sea itself, and on the other side, the white wall of cloud towers like mountains. We admire the clouds and watch how they form and change forms, faces, and figures, and pass again. The changing, the coming and going touches us strangely.

Monday
Drove in the truck to Hereford via Pontypool. On the drive back, collision with a passenger car near Pandy. A new experience. A Bobby in action! He records the case. Return at 15:00. Don't feel quite up to snuff. I suppose I caught a cold, or maybe it was only the unfriendly rumbling of the truck.

With these dry words my Ruperra journal breaks off. The long expected but nonetheless sudden end had come. I had to leave Ruperra, and what was much harder, I had to leave Greenmeadow.

The weary and frustrating assembly lines from camp to camp started crawling at long last to load us on the Channel boat to go home.

In all the months to come, the Reeses did not want to lose touch with me. But as only relatives were allowed to write to a POW, they decided to make me their nephew, and I acquired what I had never had before: an uncle and an aunt. In my journal I had always tried to fool the authorities in a game that was more imaginary than necessary. Now Mr. W. J. B. Rees, Councillor, was quite willing to lie and defy an inhuman bureaucracy.

England

Camp 685 Long Marston Near Stratford on Avon

June 28, 1946
Now I sit in the clean workroom of Long Marston Camp, near Stratford. How suddenly it all happened. On the morning of the 26th, suddenly, a truck arrived with 20 men to relieve us. A heavy blow. I just had time to write a letter to Jonba. We couldn't meet that Wednesday as we had planned, and it was hard to say good-bye to the Reeses. It really was hard to leave the paradise and to walk up the meadow again and see the dear old people wave goodbye. When I'm looking back at it now, I feel sad. Damned captivity.

> *Abschied von Ruperra*
> *So leb denn wohl, du Stätte stiller Stunden,*
> *Die ich in deiner Wälder Traum verbracht.*
> *Lebt wohl, ihr Menschen, die ich hier gefunden,*
> *Die mit mir fühlten, die mit mir gelacht.*

At 14:00 Mr. Evans drove us to Chepstow. Barbed wire—an evening of mass living and in the lost freedom somebody will be sitting, reading my letter. I was glad when we left Chepstow the next morning; frisking. Railroad Station, Gloucester, Stratford. Divided in three groups, I am in the second one. Long Marston. The area is terribly desolate. Oh beautiful Wales, where are your valleys? Oh last Sunday, where is the sun of our happy friendship. I could go on writing like this about the lost beauty and the peace. Now we're lying behind barbed wire, at the end of a widely spread-out equipment park. Tractors, ammunition boxes, without feeling—a dead landscape. Only back there, a ridge of mountains. How often have I, in the few hours that I've been here, sent my longing thoughts up there. The first bright moment in this desert was the English class last night. An English Sergeant is giving it and doing a very good job. They don't need interpreters here, but I don't want my English to get rusty. Today, work for the first time. Nailing boxes. Clean work. A long march to the workplace. I'm rather tired, but hope to get used to it soon. It's not easy, but it had to be, and in a week from now I will see it all differently.

July 5, 1946
Yesterday, English classes again with the Jewish Sergeant whose wife is from Vienna. Today I bought a marvellous large English dictionary (Cassells). I was still nailing wooden ammunition cases while reciting with appropriately heavy stresses:

> *Tomorrow and tomorrow and tomorrow*
> *Creeps in this petty pace from day to day*
> *To the last syllable of recorded time*
> *And all our yesterdays have lighted fools their way to dusty death*
> *Out, out brief candle. Life is but a walking shadow,*
> *A poor player that struts and frets his hour upon the stage*
> *and then is heard no more.*
> *'tis a tale of sound and fury signifying nothing.*

My letters home must have reflected the letdown after Wales. Ilse wrote to Long Marston:

> Just when I am most convinced of your return and already arrange homecoming celebrations I get a letter from you

that pushes me back with you into one of those awful camps. ...Reading your letters I don't see a person behind barbed wire but a free human being whose eyes have drunk the beauty of the world and will go on drinking it [...] I can imagine a Horst nailing boxes but I also know that your soul will not be harmed by it. [...]

A few days ago your classmate Burkhart came back from Paris where he was a POW. He had a pretty rough time of it. So many are still not back. One doesn't even think about them any more. Life goes on.

July 7, 1946

Last night we heard a rather mediocre concert on records. Marvellous evening. From the meadows beyond the barbed wire, a resiny scent comes drifting to us. —My explorations around Ruperra Castle had given me courage—*I wait until it's getting dark. Pulling the loose strands of barbed wire apart, I slip out. Then, like a dream: in the west the half moon, rising slowly, grows brighter and brighter as the evening sun dims and fades away. The grain stands high—a jump across the street and soon the moonlight on the other side that is shimmering on the grain stalks receives me. A pond glistens in the silver light—on and on up to the highest point. Again, a road crosses the way. On the other side, I suddenly hear steps swishing through the hay—coughing—pretty close. I quickly turn right and dive behind the next hedge. Now uphill; a garden of fruit trees; cows, startled out of sleep, rear up; the edge of the wood—pitch black. Suddenly, before me, a bright path glistens in my companion's pure light. Steep uphill. I stand in a new field of grain, and there are the masts that I had taken as my goal while I was still standing in the valley where the others are asleep, not knowing how beautiful the world is. I climb over the low fence—and am enchanted. Around me the waving sea of the grain, which passes in front of me and closes again around my hips. Over there, the forest with its dreamy wind in the trees. On, only on, through the waves to the other end. Finally I stand still. There in the distance, a string of lights, and then the wandering beam of a car, but nowhere a mountain as high as the one I am standing on. Around me a beautiful divine loneliness. Through the branches of the tree on which I'm leaning, the stars are glistening; I'm happy. Sacred joy of infinity. I climb back down through pools of light.*

It was like being back in Wales again.

I translated my pathetically inadequate "Abschied von Ruperra..." All the poetry I had heard and read had not made me a poet.

Goodbye to Ruperra

Farewell then, place of quiet hours
That I have spent in the dream of your woods
Farewell, you people whom I found there
Who shared my sorrows and my happy moods.

The next day I took part in the Catholic service. Actually only to see how far we can get in touch with civilians. I'll never go again. But I couldn't help having to take part in the theatricals, kneeling down and all that. And the ringing of the bells. And the worst, the English priest spoke only very little English. It wasn't worth the time to march to the service. I just hoped to find a way to get my letter to Jonba posted. Wrote a card to Mr. Rees tonight.

It was not just my determination to keep my English up that made me write to Greenmeadow and hope for answers. I was again in camps, and with every change the crowd changed, and none could be as congenial as was our baking crew at Ruperra. It was, above all, the constant waiting to go home at last that made one edgy and frustrated. And those final four months dragged as if they would never end. With every camp, the distance between me and Greenmeadow grew in miles and in thought. But I was delighted with every letter from there—and that in spite of the increased regularity in the mail from Austria. With these letters Wales stayed with me through all the other camps, and even afterwards in Austria. The letters convey the personalities of my Welsh friends much better than my words could, and they reveal the special kind of bond that had formed between us and that has made me write this tribute to them.

July 14, 1946
Still no mail. And all of last week, the same kind of work. Yesterday, a good American movie which I looked at again. I was pleased that I understood much more of the plot the second time. The title of the movie was "It's a Date." The most beautiful part, the ending. Schubert's Ave Maria sung in a beautiful voice.

No news from Rees nor Jonba. The letter to Jonba still hasn't left the camp.

A few days ago Mr. Hack, the Jewish teacher, who had conducted the course but was demobilized on Saturday, gave me a copy of Marlowe's Dr. Faust. *I was very pleased and I have to write him a letter of thanks. Mr. Hack, 60 Crescent, London W2.* I had left home with Goethe's *Faust* in my pocket, and returned with Marlowe's—a significant exchange in the light of Germany's recent catastrophe. I had lost my *Faust* in one of the camps, but, as my journals prove, I had returned to it again and again, read the play with others, heard lectures about it, saw scenes performed. I don't remember what I got out of it all. I suspect it was the beauty of the language, the familiar lines, many of which I had memorized, and, considering the usual drift of literary lectures in the camps, that heroic Germanness that Faust was supposed to personify, the striving of the German soul etc. which redeemed him in spite of his pact with the devil. Marlowe's *Faust* goes to hell. I am sure Mr. Hacks knew why he gave me that version of the old German legend that was more appropriate to our time.

July 16, 1946
First success of my inquiry about my request to get to an Austrian camp. One wants proof of my nationality. All I had was a letter from Mother. I hope it's enough. Finally, a letter to Jonba is on its way.

July 21, 1946
Last night, quite unexpectedly, I received a friendly letter from Mr. Rees. They wrote me the same day I left and used my real name to ensure delivery! So far only Viv had called me Horst.

    Mr. Horst Jarka
    B-302398   18 July, 1946.
    No.6 Camp (E.S.C.D.)
    685 G. P. W. W. Comp.
    Long Marston, Stratford-on-Avon

    My dear Horst,
    Your P.c. bearing the date 6-7-46, was delivered here this morning and for it I thank you. We, too, were longing to hear from you. The "farewell gate" would make an excellent and lasting picture—the tall one proclaiming, in its way, past days of ancient splendour; and the other, the opposite in colour and height—days that are more likely to continue. Viv was here on Saturday last and alone she climbed the heights for the spellbound-panoramic view. She told us she had received a letter from your good Mother. If you are allowed freedom, we should be glad to see you. How are you off for reading matter? Shall I send you that Shakespeare that was presented to me by my Australian friends? Or any other

book of my small collection? I passed through historic Stratford some years ago on my way to Lincolnshire on a visit to Albert, who was then Vicar of Sempringham in that delightful county. Some very old, dated, houses came within view-one, I think, showed the date of creation to be 1473! You will be interested to hear that Dilly caught and killed a jay yesterday-feathers enclosed-attached. Rain again today, and temperature gone down-much against the hay harvest. With our love, your affectionate Uncle and Aunt,

Ernie looked in last evening.

Another surprise today. The camp commander told me that Holtzinger and I will be transferred to Camp 203! Finally! I hope it's an Austrian camp and the longed-for direction homeward.

July 23, 1946
Finally, the first letter from Mother to this address. Very short and no mention of Jonba. Yesterday, to my great joy, a letter from Viv herself. Just wrote a letter to her and Uncle and Aunty Rees, which I leave with Biskup to mail for me. (He, too, was a POW but had a job driving a lorry and could get out of the camp) Tomorrow at eight off to Derby, that is Martin and I. Wanted to write in my journal again, but was busy writing letters all evening.

Newport, Mon.
20.7.46

Dear Horst,

I was out at Greenmeadow today and your aunt and uncle were so happy to have received news from you that they gave me your address and I am sitting down at once to write to you.

Where shall I begin? At the beginning? Yes. Back in thought to that day when you were forced to leave us. I was at Greenmeadow that evening and the silence, stillness, and emptiness that we felt as if some one had died. So you can imagine now, how great was our joy! how unbounded our exaltation! Horst, how your ears must have burned because we recalled all our talking, laughing, thinking and our total disregard of time which always passed by much too quickly.

A week ago today I received a letter from your mother. Her letters are always an inspiration to me for they radiate a sweet patience and indomitable courage. ...We have been wondering if it is possible for us to visit you. How wonderful would be her joy if I could write and tell her I had seen you and spoke to you. She is naturally anxious for you for she has not seen you for years... I trust I shall be permitted to see you.

Oh yes, I must tell you of my expedition to the little hill. I was most astonished to find that the wood rising steeply to the top had grown gigantic ferns and brambles. Yes, literally gigantic–they towered high above my head. There was no vestige of a path, all semblance had been entirely obliterated. I scrambled and plunged headlong into it getting deeper and deeper every moment but there was nothing to do but push valiantly forward. Looking upwards I espied a gap in the trees and thinking it would quickly bring me to the top and to the open space I swayed and struggled towards it. Ah! poor me, when I had accomplished this feat of endurance it was only to find an ever expanding land of ferns and brambles. Once more I plodded on and to my great surprise quite suddenly I stepped into the path at last. How you would have laughed to behold the spectacle I now presented! I did not care I was not even aware of it at the time but with a swing now I strode gaily forward. I stayed at the top for quite a while, thinking, remembering many things. My experience, however, taught me to seek out another way down to the road on the return journey. I was pleased to discover quite a good path which led me out of the wood back to my starting point.

Reading through my letter I am struck that my being trapped in the wood is a good analogy of your present life. Let us trust that you will be granted freedom just as unexpectedly and a chance to study at the University where you really belong. I know that whatever menial task you are set to do you will do quietly, patiently but you will keep your heart and mind well above your condition, you will live in

the highest and best part of you keeping the star of your being in true position and ever shining.
    I have every faith in you. God bless you, Horst,
               All my love, Vivo

CAMP 23, SUDBURY

July 26, 1946
Sudbury, near Derby. Camp 23. Yesterday morning we left Long Marston. On the train we meet again two Austrians, who, like us, are guarded by a sentry; changed train in Birmingham. Meet more POWs on the way to the same camp. Also, in Derby, where we wait for two hours, and arrive in Camp 23 with about one hundred and fifty of us. Frisking, bathing, delousing powder pumps. Exactly as in Kempton Park two years ago. After bathing, I suddenly meet Krainz Sepp. The camp is very clean, but also scanty about the food. Most important, however, is that it looks like repatriation. Rumours are favourable. We're supposed to stay 14 to 28 days here and then... I can't believe it. It would be too good to be true. And yet, perhaps...

July 28, 1946
Day before yesterday, five letters from Mother and four from Ilse. Mother received the package from Jones and Ilse rides her bike to St. Gilgen for summer vacation. I'll try to be released there. The Salzburg Festival, too, can be expected soon. Will I be at home on my birthday??

July 31, 1946
Still in Camp 23. Getting home won't be quite as fast. And actually it is still quite difficult to prepare oneself for returning home. Obviously, all my thoughts go ahead to meet Ruth on Lake Wolfgang where I also hope to see Ilse. Has she changed? From her last letters I see her intellectual superiority. Also, when I see the other academic people here in the camp, I observe that I am intellectually far behind them. Ilse writes, in one of her last letters, "Yes, I am afraid of life." –Yes, I, too, feel the same, but I have such powerful confidence in my energy to overcome everything. My inferiority feelings have their cause in the consciousness of my social inferiority. I am happy about Ilse's belief in loneliness in her last letter. She will probably be able to understand better how I felt when I was still at home. I see that from her last letters about our being together again – "Perhaps we will say nothing because it will be too much."

August 1, 1946
Today I made friends with a very knowledgeable Swiss in our hut. (He was determined

to be the first of his schoolmates to own an automobile!) *We studied English together. Above all, the time passes quickly in a nice and useful way. It's good to be busy especially since in this camp our stomachs have been empty more or less all of the time. In the afternoon, a very nice letter from Ilse. She writes "I would love best to get on my bike and peddle on and on until I'm in Great Britain." It's really time that we get home. Sunday, we're supposed to take another step toward home. I hope I can start thinking optimistically again.*
How strange life is. The same mail that brought me Ilse's letter brought Franz the definite news of his fiance's wedding. He had believed in that girl for two years.

August 2, 1946
In the evening we lie on the camp meadow. From the radio come the well-known tunes of Viennese waltzes. All my thoughts fly home with the clouds. Tomorrow the decision will be made whether or not we're going to get away from here and head home. Anyway the food here is better than at home. But what do I care about the food? All I want is that they send us home. Uncle Rees again sent me a very warm letter. How far away those days seem now. My letter from Stratford he apparently never got.

Greenmeadow
Llanfedwy, St. Melan's
Cardiff
July 27, 1946

My dear boy,

Knowing your admiration for the beauties of Nature, let me tell you about the Blue Clematis. Its gorgeous blooms by the hundred, are making a magnificent display among the painted petals of its less showy neighbours. And while it is in my mind, and you may be glad to know, Avon, the British word for river, is pronounced Ah von. And now I will try to describe an incident that took place not far from here some little time ago. A devoted family trio were about to be disintegrated. Hands had been firmly clasped, the hearts were fettered. They now came to the parting of the ways, and waving their last "farewell." Then with growing distance between them came the extreme trial–disappearance. The muffled drums were beating to the mete of heaving sighs as each moved onward to their respective destination! He gave us of his best, and the thought of that best sweetens the memory. 'As I write I look towards the basket of beautiful roses, and give a glance towards the old armchair in which so many of our dear ones have rested. The voice of the hour bell echoes in the old hall. Sunshine without and the white clouds borne away by the westerly wind preparing us to expect more rain! With our love through joys and sorrow.

Auntie Mary and Uncle William

[Enclosures.] The clematis is seen to the best advantage from high up among the dark coloured leaves of the Rowan tree forming the bower.

My little children, let us not love in words, neither with the tongue, but in deed and truth. Epistles St. John iii. 17-18. William Wilberforce comes to mind now, whose name stands out in English literature. Our last Council Meeting before the vacation takes place on the 31st of this month. We assemble again on the first Wed. in Sep.

August 3, 1946
Last night I was moved to a different compound. Here, in Camp E, it is far more unfriendly than up there in Compound F. Yesterday, I bought a new book from a Canadian for twenty cigarettes: The Arabian Nights. *The Canadian POWs, of which we have so many in this camp, look awful with their "general's" red stripes down their legs and a big red moon on their backs.*

August 9, 1946
I'm sitting in the huge Nissen hut, the so-called leisure hall, and working on my translation of Marlowe's Doctor Faustus *which I will give Ilse as a present.* [She never saw it.] *I was able to buy some cake today, so, at least on my birthday, I wasn't hungry. And I had hoped to be on board ship by now and home by the full moon. I am still a little of a pessimist. Last night petty bargaining with cake and cigarettes. It's good, at least, that we Austrians in the camp can hope that this mass existence won't last too much longer. I bought myself a birthday present in the form of a fountain pen for nineteen shillings, but I'm sure I got cheated. But I enjoy it. I am glad to have it.*

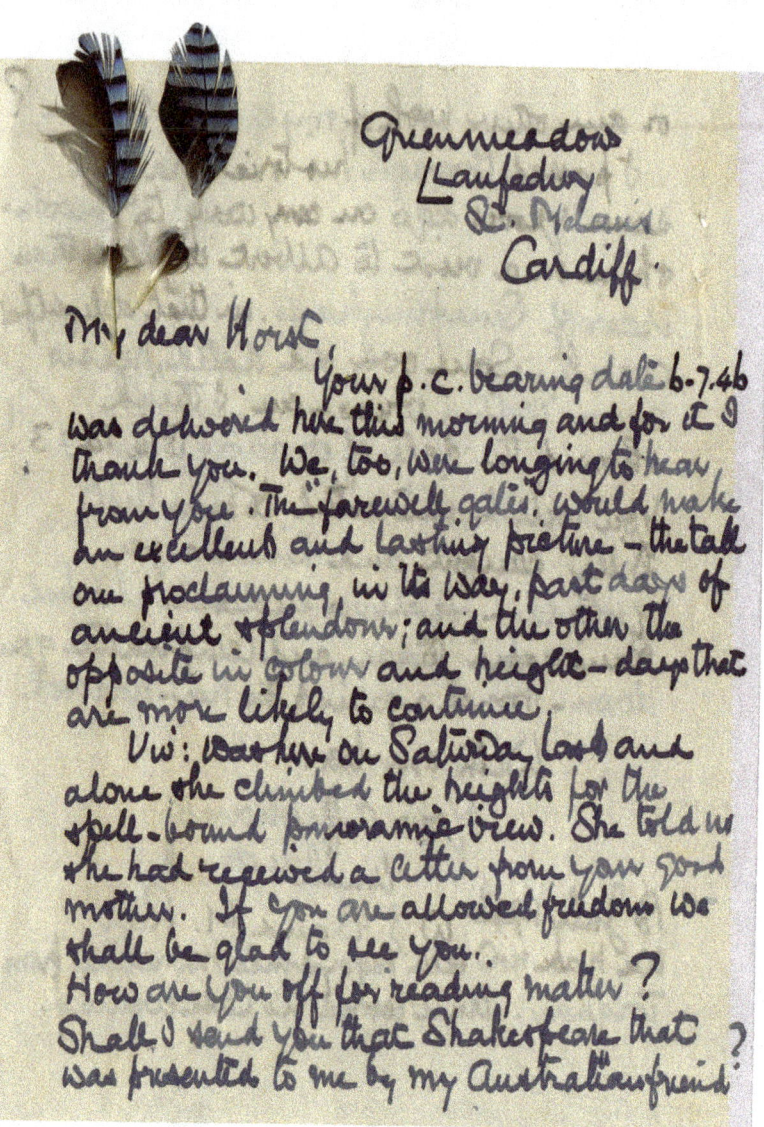

Letter to Horst from "Uncle William," written with his quill with blue jay feathers attached.

or any other book of my small collection? I passed through historic Shatford some years ago on my way to Lincolnshire on a visit to Albert who was then Vicar of Sempringham. in that delightful county. Some very old, dated, houses came within view — one, I think showed the date of creation to be 1473!

You will be interested to hear that "Dilly" caught and killed a jay Yesterday — feathers enclosed – attached. Rain again today, and temperature gone down — French against the hay-harvest.

With our love.
Your affectionate
Uncle + Aunt

8 July 1946 W. J. B and M. Rees

We have not seen Peggy since her return from Torquay. Ernie looked in last evening.

August 10, 1946

Damn shitty weather. It's been raining since the morning incessantly and the rain brings chilly air. At home in Austria it's the height of summer and Ilse might be swimming in one of the mountain lakes. The morning I spent again in the stinky un-cosy and, of course, crowded "leisure hall." In the afternoon, I go to my bunk and sleep.

> "The day is cold and dark and dreary.
> It rains and the wind is never weary."

I only hope to get mail soon from Uncle William and Viv.

Letter from Viv...

> ...Uncle William finds he has to read your letters before he carries them into the house... In the afternoon the sun was shining, and I decided to climb our little hill when who should arrive but Ernie. So I sat down again and talked—It was so much like those evenings when you were here that you seemed once more there with us. I was often drawn to look at the big chair beside the hearth. Memories crowded in and a peaceful, quiet happiness filled the room ...Horst, where are you? Soon I shall know...

August 11, 1946

Wrote a letter to Mother and an English one to Greenmeadow, card to Ruth and one to Ilse. In the afternoon I received a letter from Mother with very kind words about Viv and a letter from Auntie and Uncle Rees. In it were a birthday card and these two poems, which Uncle had copied on a piece of paper with his quill.

> I know not how, but as I count,
> The beads of former years,
> Old laughter catches in my throat
> With the very feel of tears.
> So live so love, so use that fragile hour,
> That when the dark hand of the shining power,
> Shall one from another, wife or husband take,
> The poor survivor may not weep and wake.
>
> R. L. Stevenson

> But, oh, for the hand
> Just to hold for a space,
> For a moment to stand
> In the light of thy face.
> Translate "then" to "now"
> To hear Is it thou?
> And reply "It is I."
> Then I could wait,
> Ah: then I could wait
> Long and late.
>
>   Richard le Gallienne

August 16, 1946

A long letter from Ilse tonight. Salzburg–picture postcard included–! Salzburg! Glorious city. Festival. And Ilse has two tickets for Everyman on August 25th and doesn't know whom to go with! She is writing about dancing and farm boys and merriment–oh yes, Horst, you missed a lot and maybe Ilse might like it more to dance with a lad than to walk side by side with a taciturn POW–but no–if I could only be there! Also letter from Uncle Rees. He has written his Member of Parliament about repatriation of Austrian POWs, and he sent me a copy of his letter. Included were a few lines from Cornwall, which pleased me very much. Viv also sent packages to Mother again.

Uncle William, following his quote from St. John's Epistle, had been thinking of some way in which he could actively help me and other POWs. He had written to his MP about the repatriation of Austrian POWs, and sent me the official card from the House of Commons:

>   July 7, 46
>
> Mr. Ungoed Thomas has the honour to acknowledge the receipt of your communication of the [no date]—the subject matter of which is receiving his attention.

Nothing came of that but Uncle William did not give up and tried a different route with the result that he included in his letter to me:

> From Prehendary W.L. Cottrell
> The King's Chapel of the Savoy
> W.C.2

10. Aug. 46

My dear William

It was so good to see your writing again and I am interested in what you say about your Austrian friend. Much as my sentiment is for these POWs, I fear I can do nothing. I think your MP will be able to ensure you that there is a general outcry that these men whose crime lay in being loyal to their own country (as we indeed are to ours) shall soon be allowed to go back home. I don't think this will be long delayed for there is a general public feeling that this should be. I hope so and I hope it will mean a speedy return for your friend. [...]

I am glad to hear that you are both well and that you too are active in public affairs. There's been much water under the bridge since 1909-16. Perhaps I did not tell you that I ended my prison service on March 31st last. Hence my change over to other circles. [...]

All my best wishes to my old friend and his sister,

Yours sincerely
W. L. Cottrell

A clergyman who was taking care of prisoners could be an influential ally in what Uncle considered a just cause. He didn't tell me whether he tried once more to get the attention of his MP. Cottrell's hopeful remark about the "public feeling" might have reassured him and, to reassure me, he sent along a newspaper clipping in support of that sentiment:

Professor Joad

Do you think that our present treatment and continued retention of German prisoners is right?

No. When all is said and done they are human beings and have a right to be treated as such; that is to say, they have a right to be treated as ends in themselves with rights of their own and not merely as instruments to serve our ends, and to fulfil purposes other than their own.

Also, when all is said and done, they are not slaves and have a right not to be treated as slaves.

Let me define a slave as a person who can't determine whom he is to work for or on what conditions, or for how many hours; or how much in the way of wages he is to receive, adding that he can't marry whom he pleases and doesn't know when, if ever, he will be released.

Now, look at the lot of the German prisoners. Here they are, still in an enemy country more than a year after the war. Most of them are worried to death about their families; they cannot send gifts of food to their families although their families often send gifts to them; although their employers pay the trade union rate for their work, they themselves receive only 1½ d. a day; above all they don't know when, if ever, they are going to be allowed to go back to Germany.

This treatment is neither moral nor Christian. If Christianity and morality mean nothing to us, what about expediency? In effect, we are manufacturing a lot of cynical, disgruntled men out of repentant sinners who were at one time prepared to feel and even to confess disillusionment with Hitler and his methods and, as a consequence, were ripe for conversion to a belief in the virtues of Christianity and the practice of democracy.

Many of them, indeed, suffered a real change of heart. But now, more than a year after the end of the war, they are losing faith in the ideals of decency and democracy that we professed to put before them.

"You say," they complain in effect, "that Hitler's Germany was a slave State and that we Germans treated members of other nationalities like slaves, putting them to forced labour. In what respect, then, do you do different. You say that we offended against the rights of man by putting prisoners up in camps without any definite charge for indefinite periods so that they never knew when they would be released. Once again, how do you do different?"

One other thing. It is costing us 80,000,000 pounds a year to maintain the Germans in our zone at the moment, partly because Germany cannot get on its feet again as an economic unit. Why not? Because in large areas of Germany nearly all the male population between the ages of 20 and 35 is missing. Our prisoners are mostly young, virile men who are badly needed not only to re-establish the economic life of Germany but also, if we are wise in our treatment of them, a democratic state of Germany.

At the time I had no idea who Dr. Joad was nor did I know the extent of his popularity. I was probably impressed by his "English" fairness and completely overlooked his incredible comparison of our condition as POWs in Britain to that in the Nazi concentration camps. Apparently, even after the Bergen Belsen trials in British Courts the Holocaust had not yet penetrated the consciousness of the public, not to mention that of a well-known Professor of Philosophy.

August 17, 1946
At rollcall tonight the names of all Austrians were read, tomorrow to Compound B, and on Monday we leave Camp 23! Finally, the time has come. Perhaps I'll be home on the 25th after all.

P.S. Viv received the letter which I left behind me in Camp 685 on August 9th! Better late than never! Now I have hardly the peace of mind to read, and have only one thought—fast, fast—if only time would really fly. I hope they don't take anything away from me. But then, who cares? Only to get home! Home—

Home was getting closer, and so were the contacts between home and Greenmeadow. The connections between "our relatives in Wales that had been interrupted by the war" were finally restored. Mother had joined our game.

Kierling, July 28, 1946

My beloved son

How sure I was that you would be home for your birthday! But this won't happen and perhaps you will be hungry on that day. But be patient and look towards the sun as Viv expressed it so beautifully. What a dear person she is, and I think she is the only one who does not laugh at my ideas about the healing moulds. She has ordered a book about it for me. I am glad that you can converse with her; your English must be pretty fluent by now. I am

Professor JOAD

? Do you think that our present treatment and continued retention of German prisoners is right?

NO. When all is said and done they are human beings and have a right to be treated as such; that is to say, they have a right to be treated as ends in themselves with rights of their own and not merely as instruments to serve our ends, and to fulfil purposes other than their own.

Also, when all is said and done, they are not slaves and have a right not to be treated as slaves.

Let me define a slave as a person who can't determine who he is to work for or on what conditions, or for how many hours; or how much in the way of wages he is to receive, adding that he can't marry whom he pleases and doesn't know when, if ever, he will be released.

☆

NOW, look at the lot of the German prisoners. Here they are, still in an enemy country more than a year after the war. Most of them are worried to death about their families; they can't send gifts of food to their families although their families often send gifts to them; although their employers pay the trade union rate for their work, they themselves receive only 1½d. a day; above all, they don't know when, if ever, they are going to be allowed to go back to Germany.

NOT MORAL OR CHRISTIAN

This treatment is neither moral nor Christian. If Christianity and morality mean nothing to us, what about expediency? In effect, we are manufacturing a lot of cynical, disgruntled men out of repentant sinners who were at one time prepared to feel and even to confess disillusionment with Hitler and his methods and, as a consequence, were ripe for conversion to a belief in the virtues of Christianity and the practice of democracy.

☆

MANY of them, indeed, suffered a real change of heart. But now, more than a year after the end of the war, they are losing faith in the ideals of decency and democracy that we professed to put before them.

"You say," they complain in effect, "that Hitler's Germany was a slave State and that we Germans treated members of other nationalities like slaves, putting them to forced labour. In what respect, then, do you do different? You say that we offended against the rights of man by shutting prisoners up in camps without any definite charge for indefinite periods so that they never knew when they would be released. Once again, how do you do different?"

One other thing. It is costing us £80,000,000 a year to maintain the Germans in our zone at the moment, partly because Germany cannot get on its feet again as an economic unit. Why not? Because in large areas of Germany nearly all the male population between the ages of 20 and 35 is missing. Our prisoners are mostly young, virile men who are badly needed not only to re-establish the economic life of Germany, but also, if we are wise in our treatment of them, a democratic state of Germany.

The Actual Newspaper Clipping Sent to Horst by "Uncle William"

now corresponding with her. The other day I received a letter from some English office informing me that a parcel containing coffee had been posted to me but that the export of coffee was not permitted. A kind person's thoughtfulness was thus thwarted.

On Saturday Viv visited Uncle and Auntie who live near Newport, and she took my letter along, and everybody was happy about it. Only one person was missing to make the happiness complete…Nothing can surprise me any more, my son. Will you teach me English? But you are too tough for me. I remember that from our Latin lessons. Viv sent me verses and sayings for your collection. Be patient. As long as we live we are slaves, all people are in one way or another.

Card to Uncle William.

My only concrete "cultural achievement" in Camp 23 seems to have been that I acquired a Modern Library copy of Daphne du Maurier's *Rebecca* and *The Arabian Nights*.

Camp 186, Colchester

August 20, 1946

Monday morning we left Sudbury-Darby and were on the train til six p.m. The ride Sudbury–Rugby–Cambridge–Ipswich–Colchester. In Colchester we left the train and marched through the town which has a clean small-town character. After three miles we finally reached our goal: Camp 186. We were pretty bushed since, in the morning, we had received only a small ration for the march. Here we were frisked again. The camp is very clean and in general the atmosphere is rather favourable, as far as repatriation is concerned. The shipping port is supposed to be not very far from here, and even if the food is scanty again, the hope that we won't stay too long is great. In Colchester there were some very beautiful Tudor houses.

August 21, 1946
Berechurch Hall Camp.
Unofficial letter to Viv and Uncle William, to be mailed by the driver of the work team. Perhaps I'll get some reply too. If there's any mail here at all, and if I'm not at home by that time. Every day, new POWs arrive, most of them in their newly issued uniforms.

August 22, 1946
Just talked to Arthur Pichler. He was in High School in Klosterneuburg, one class below me, so he joined the army in '44. I had hoped he had graduated with Ilse, but unfortunately he did not. He was an Air Force Auxiliary in Vienna. We spoke about the professors and the school. How far back is all that–??!

August 24, 1946
Colchester. I'm sitting in the cosy reading room of the camp and read HG. Wells' Machiavelli. *It's very hard for me to read, that is to understand and I'm running through the book, catching at least the plot. Perhaps it would be better to read something else and yet, I don't want to give up. I find it hard to concentrate right now. The prospects of being repatriated are rather dim at the moment. I'm waiting for mail from Viv or Uncle William.*

August 25, 1946
Lying on the sports ground, tired Ilse is in Salzburg seeing Everyman. *How could I ever have been so optimistic?*

August 26, 1946
My POW-time seems to end as it began, at least, as far as the food is concerned, which is rather meager in this transit camp. We have to get up rather early for roll call. I'm spending my time in the reading room.

August 28, 1946
Found magnificent words by Shelley:

> *"Ode to the West Wind."*
> *Oh, lift me as a wave, a leaf, a cloud!*
> *If all upon the thorns of life, I bleed!*
> *A heavy weight of hours has chained and bow'd*
> *One too like thee–, tameless, and swift and proud!*

August 31, 1946
This afternoon I was transferred to Camp D. Some of us stayed behind. Great excitement– hope that we're going to get out of here soon. I'm sitting in the reading room and just finished The Tempest.

September 3, 1946
Camp 186

This morning before roll call, my name was suddenly called. I was to go to the Interpreter

Officer. My first thought was that something was wrong with the mail from Viv or Uncle William. There were also some other officers present, and I was getting ready for an interrogation. (There are some blokes from the Secret Service, London, here to interrogate us—a good sign by the way—indicating our imminent departure from here.) How magically my tense excitement turned into joy: a letter from Uncle William and Auntie Mary and a very dear letter from Viv and a package from her. A real package! With a marvellous book Britain in Verse and Sketch *by Lindley Searle. The very best goodbye gift that I could imagine. How pleased I was. Now I'm sitting in the reading room.* The Pilgrim's Progress *has to wait a little, I guess, and I just dive into the letters to read them savouring every word.*

Newport Mon
26 August 1946

Dear Horst,

Your letter, for which I thank you very much, was here when I arrived home tonight. How I wish you had written to the Cornwall address. Now I'm sad wondering whether you have heard from me before leaving this country. I know now how much I have wished and hoped I would see you just once more before you had to leave. I'm deeply hurt that you must go so far away without seeing you. I, too, wish you had come to Newport on that memorable Friday. But the thought of you one day returning buoys me up with joy. You know how great will be your welcome.

I'm not very good at saying goodbye, and now that you are off, I'm a little too sad. Do you understand? You know, I wish for all that is best for you. I shall look forward eagerly to receiving a letter from you from Austria. We shall then be able to write more freely. Please do not forget that I'm your friend, any books, etc., Horst, you know, I shall count it a privilege to be given the opportunity to help you. I trust you will like my little parting gift. When I came across it, I could not resist it. It was so just exactly right for you. I did not send it before because I hadn't your address and I wanted to show it your Aunt and Uncle, but now it must go for there is still just the chance that you will receive it while still in this country. I'm still trying to send parcels to your Mother. I have written to the Board of Trade and the Returned Letter

Office, but so far, I have received no reply. I do not give up easily and your Aunt and Uncle will help me, too.

I've just received a card from them which says they will be so pleased to see me on Saturday and we shall have such lots to talk about. I shall visit our little hill and place my hands upon the stone. May Providence guide you, Horst, and bless you.

With all my love, Vivo

PS If you have received the note paper and envelopes from me, I have hidden some stamps inside of the envelopes.

23 Aug. 1946

Our beloved John,

Your very kind letter dated 20th Aug. was handed in here a few moments ago. In it you would have us know that a letter had been dispatched by you from Sudbury on the 11th of Aug. This Letter has not reached us, and why? The song says—"Wait a little longer." ….

> "Thoughts of other days and happy
> Roll their plaintive voice along."

Glad we were to understand by your letter that you are alright. You don't realize the pleasure your companionship was giving us. May you live long and soon be once again amid your familiar surroundings and your dear ones—there will be joy! Sometimes I experience a break in my slumbers in the middle of the night. I listen in the deafening silence in case a pedestrian has lost his way—as travellers some-times do—but, with the stillness unbroken I drop off again. Need I tell you, John, of the hearts' yearnings that have been experienced in this solitary abode, set in the midst of so much natural beauty—as a result of the "recruited" Angel being torn from us—are we likely to forget the severance of the morning of the 26th of June 1946? No, emphatically "No!"

> But under each rank Wrong
> Somewhere there lies the root of Right.

In order to prepare the unsuspecting wayfarer for possibilities, what do you say, John, to this notice–

Travellers, beware!
This may be Beelzebub's lair!

Here is a true story told me in the now distant past by my Oxford friend of "Dog and Broom" fame: In those far-off days a Mr. Seddon was Landaff Diocesan Architect. One day Mrs. S. called on some friends, and the maid who admitted her, not quite certain of the name, announced her as Mrs. Satan at the drawing-room door. When the lady got in among her friends she said, "I expect you are glad my husband didn't come with me!"

Your melodious voice frees itself from the receptive cells as my eye follows the route of your guided pen over the recording sheet. Thank you again for the treasured lines. [...] "Dinky" and "Dilly" are alright. Owing to the intrusion of the liquid element through a few leaks in the roof I fixed up the long ladder against the house, and lighter ladder at the roof angle. As I was using the trowel, to my surprise, "Dilly" was beside me. She did enjoy being so high up. I am glad you are allowed to retain possession of your books. More in the next letter, I hope.

With my love, Your affectionate Uncle William

The books! My treasures! To help me along with my English Uncle William had given me *The Etymological Spelling-Book and Expositor. An Introduction to the Spelling, Pronunciation, and Derivation of the English Language* by Henry Butter, London 1885 (434th edition). It is lying before me now, and on the flyleaf, in ink so faded that it is white against the darkened background I can just make out the handwriting: William John(?) Beynon Rees, Green Meadow, Cefn Mably, Cardiff 1888 and he could very well have used this book as schoolboy himself. The handwriting is that of an older student, so he may have been born before 1880, and in 1946 he may have been in his early seventies. Other book presents from him were *Essays and Essayists*, Compiled and Edited by Henry Newbolt, Thomas & Nelson & Sons, London 1929, (1925); *Prose of Our Time*. Edited by A. J. J. Ratcliff, Thomas Nelson & Sons, London 1932 (1931). Somewhere I had also acquired *First Aid in English* and a *Everybody's*

Pocket Dictionary. The big *Cassell's Dictionary* I had bought in Long Marsten had been certified as my property by a Major, Commanding Officer 685 P.W.W. Company. To be sure that my most treasured books *The Golden Treasury* and the Ifor Evans might also be safe from confiscation I had already at Ruperra taken precautions: on the typewriter I had manufactured my own official looking label, created an Interpreter Officer of POW Camp 186 Camp and signed for him: Drew. Cpt.

In all the other books I had written my name and POW-number; nobody in all the frisking crews I had to pass ever looked at them, and I still have all of them. I confess that I also have two books that I did not even try to smuggle out of the country. As reward for my strenuous service as librarian at the Ruperra Bakery I had appropriated the Army Shakespeare and *The Tower of London*. Because of the stamps in them—one of them said: Services Library. County Borough. Newport. Mon. With Gratitude from the Citizens—I could not very well claim them as my property, so I had taken them to Ernie's cottage the evening when we heard Marlene Dietrich, and asked him to mail them after me to Austria. Had Mother not written in her letter on July 26: "Are you allowed to take books with you when repatriation gets serious? I love to read Shakespeare's History Plays."

Another letter from Uncle!

"The Verdant Pastures"
Surrounded by beautiful trees
Your Home in Wales
August 28, 1946

Our beloved John,

The gentle breezes have borne away the obscuring clouds and thankful we are that you are homeward bound! We trust that you will find your dear Mother and Sister and all old friends quite well. How delighted they will be at the re-union! We always feel that you are near us, more so, when we are perusing your lovely letters, which we do as often as we can. Your touching lines have found a deep, and an abiding place in our hearts. Yes, old man, true are the words—"Even this shall pass away," and, equally true is the fact that the disturbing effects of the memorable 26th of June still linger in their fulfilment! The little we were able to do for you could not possibly compensate for the pleasure your companionship gave us. We were to you a "spark in the night." You were to us a bright and shining star–

> "with folded arms we linger not,
> to call him back 'twas vain,
> in this, or in some other spot
> we know he'll shine again."

It was yesterday that your card written on the 16th inst. and franked on the 24th came into our possession…. Keep in mind the "Farewell Gates"–the one beside the highway, the other beside the stream, on different levels. Listen, John, here is a proverb: Better to go on wearing soiled garments than to risk clothing not thoroughly aired by the fire for in this way we are inviting discomforts for the coming year. That non-egotistic epistle of yours was admirable and shall be preserved. With my grateful thanks for happy hours, and the love of an affectionate uncle William in Wales.

September 4, 1946
Last night, letter to Viv. This morning to Auntie and Uncle.

September 5, 1946
This morning I finally managed to give my letters to the driver.

September 6, 1946
Last night, another surprise. The long letter from Cornwall, that Viv had promised has arrived. I was very pleased. She always writes so nicely. A true friend, full of warmth. In her book, I just found a sketch of the Cornwall coast, and I can well imagine her sitting there on the rocks, writing. How young she is, in spite of her grey hair which is in such a contradiction to her lively, romantic brown eyes. How quickly heart finds heart. We have known each other such a short time. We don't know anything about each other, except that we felt close from the very first moment. But isn't that everything? She could be my mother. I'm thinking of Greenmeadow, like a dream full of peace, a safe haven. That beautiful Sunday of forgetting. The last goodbye on the little bridge over the brook, and I'm still facing a puzzle.
She writes of books she has sent me and I hope I'll still get them. In fact, I wanted to write her right away, but I find myself unable to do so. Our present prospect of repatriation is

very dim. We're waiting to be interrogated and it hasn't even been decided yet whether we are to be repatriated or not. Perhaps another work camp is waiting for us. And Mother and Ilse and University are waiting for me. Yesterday I also got a letter from Mother from the 13th of August: "Why aren't you coming here, come soon to your old Mother."

September 8, 1946
Just back from the interrogation. I walked in there determined to deceive the Secret Service. But they don't send idiots for this kind of thing. He knew immediately where I stand. My attitude is quite clear: I have always had the intention of trying to understand democracy, to think myself into its system, and I found a lot of good in it. But if they keep me longer in this country, my attitude will change, and I already know that I will not hold back anything. If this interrogation chief knows human nature, he'll send me home.

I have no idea how concrete my intention of trying to understand democracy ever became. Viv mentioned in a letter that we had discussed politics before she even knew that I was interested in poetry, and Ernie might have told me why he was in the left-of-center Independent Labour Party. My "threat" showed that I had adopted Dr. Joad's argument, and I had my reasons. The Geneva Convention prohibited any political instruction by the camp authorities. Occasionally there was an article about British politics in the POW paper, like the one of Harold J. Laski, that I had translated, but I had really no idea about democracy. The last political election I remember was in 1932 when I was seven. Mother took me with her to the voting booth and, as always, she voted the Social Democratic ticket. Two years later the Austro-fascists wiped out democracy in Austria. After the tragic February uprising of the workers in 1934, Mother took me to see the shell holes in the Karl-Marx-Hof, one of the municipal housing projects of Red Vienna that had been admired by the whole world. After four years of Austro-fascist authoritarianism, Hitler marched in; I was 13. So I had never lived in a democracy. My interrogator probably understood all that from my answers, and was less interested in Austria's past than in her future, and wanted to know whether in my opinion Austria could be economically and politically independent. I knew nothing about the present situation in Austria except that it was pretty miserable and that Mother was growing potatoes and eating stinging nettles soup, and said yes, of course.

September 9, 1946
Letter to Viv, which I wrote last night, is finally off.

September 10, 1946

Last night, I came from Camp A and found, to my great joy, a letter from Viv in which she confirms receipt of my letter of September 5th. On the envelope, it said "If not deliverable, please forward to Vienna." Right now, I'm not at all confident. If only it were definite what they want to do with us. Now off to the dentist. Viv wrote of two more packages, which I haven't got yet. Tonight, I was called to the Interpreter Officer again. I went there with the joyful expectation of books. But this time, she had sent me something to eat. At first, I was somewhat disappointed, since the tomatoes on top were squashed and mouldy. But, the greatest part was ok, and I'm very happy with it. And so will be the others, Franz and Martin. There was also a very nice letter included, which again reveals to me a part of her soul. What a dear person she is.

And, of course, she played along with our uncle-aunt-nephew camouflage.

Newport, 1st September 1946

Dear Horst,

As I sit down to write to you tonight I wonder whether or not you have already departed from our shores. As I journeyed in the bus toward Greenmeadow I fell seriously to thinking that you had indeed been granted permission to take leave of your Aunt and Uncle before setting out on the homeward journey. It was not until I had at last entered the house that I became quite convinced that you were not there. You should have seen us. In a very few moments we each held one of your letters and read it. They are constantly talking about you at Greenmeadow—wouldn't John laugh at this or that, here he would say so and so and there something else and so it goes on every day. You are still a part of them and I think you always will be a part of them. I do hope you have received my letters and the books etc. Nothing of my correspondence has been returned to me and therefore my hopes that you have received all of it are rising high. I have been busy collecting a little parcel for you. I shall post it to Colchester with a note saying that, if you have left, will they please hand it over to any other prisoners at the camp. I do not know whether to post this letter to Vienna or to Colchester but have hit upon the idea of enclosing a stamped envelope addressed to Vienna and asking whoever opens the parcel to forward the letter to you.

Oh Horst, to be going home! How wonderful that must be for you! It must be impossible for you to contain yourself. Give my love to your dear Mother. Tell her I wish her to have every happiness. I know how great will be your joy when you are both together. I believe now that there is hope that I shall be able to help you. I had a long chat with a post office assistant who was strongly sympathetic and thought that I would probably be granted an export licence. They are probably checking up whether my friend is a genuine one or not. There has been such a racket now by people desiring to get rich quick that restrictions have been tightened and every parcel examined and its contents determined. There is good news too for a parcel weighing up to 11 lbs. can be posted to Austria since August 21st. But the list of restrictions is most extensive and I was at a loss to think of even one thing that I was allowed to send. However, if I am not mistaken (and I shall enquire again and copy out the list of goods which must not be sent) I can send you books and stationary etc. That is good. Isn't it? And remember we have students taking Honours German at our universities and so maybe I shall be able to get to German books you may require as well as the English perhaps even better than you will be able to get them in Austria because here there has not been such awful destruction. This goes, too, for any books your friends may require. You see, Horst, I love to help you all. You will understand why.

I shall write again and send you the suggested correction of your translation piece about Christopher Wren. You must have the quotations I wrote for you and took to Greenmeadow the Wednesday that you left us… John Keats' poem you must have in full though. I think it must be in the *Golden Treasury*. This must suffice for tonight.

God bless you, Horst

PS I quite forgot to tell you, the apples, pears and eggs are from Greenmeadow; I brought them back with me yesterday.

11 Clifton Place.
Newport, Mon:
8. 9. '46.

Dear Horst, I am happy, too! Glad that the authorities decided to hand you that parcel. By your letter I can see that some of my letters (the longest I best, I think) or a parcel containing a long letter, note paper, envelopes, stamps, three pocket editions of Shakespeare's plays, "Let the People Think", all of which printed in Penrunde have not reached you. Maybe I have written too frequently but how much more that I had were grateful I am now that the other me wish it it meant you were to receive this than planned times to send you letters which its confirmation that the book gave you joy. I knew it was the book for you at the moment I saw it. I am now no happy knowing I know you so well — that is the greatest reward I could ever receive.

Yesterday I visited Newcomen—but once more I was in dreamy mood. I did not seem to be able to get any where. Perhaps I was far away. I can't say quite how it happened

Letter to Horst from Vivian Jones, August 9, 1945

there were groups of
people in all the shops
and everywhere things seemed
to go wrong and I lost
the two that would take
me nearest to Enniscorthy
— and had to catch the
one for it Chellen. I
was not sorry for I
had not walked from
it Mullen since last
oft- November being Wednesday
and I was glad to see
again the view of
Kilpenna Castle. I left
Moakley as you had
seen it, rain-drenched
of course, but ever
more beautiful now
for the autumn tints are
beginning to colour the trees

she were happy at their
meadow reading your letters
eagerly. I am about any
good. I. Uncle William
finds he must read
your letters before he
carries them into the
house & I am the same
mine began. I read while
will standing at the door.
Oh think! what if you
have given in all!
In the afternoon the
air was showing & I
decided to think at still
the turn in just quite
going when who showed
a miner but Louie. She
insisted it had been
you — It would have
been rude to have left
her when it was just
then & so I out

down again & talked. Presently the rain descended and it continued to pour down heavily until about 8 o'clock. I left at my usual time 8.30. It was so much like those evenings I spent at Buckenham when you were there that you seemed once more there and I was often drawn down to look at the big chair beside the hearth. Memories crowded in and a peaceful, quiet happiness filled the room. Again thank you.

Deeply grateful.
Where are you? I wonder. Soon I shall know.

Your lines describing your feelings and thought as you approached the Interpreter's Office touched me very much. All the very best of luck and a pleasant journey.

All ... may have this ...

P.S. Did you receive the parcel I sent you last week?

I wonder whether they were goose eggs.

September 11, 1946
Last night I couldn't sleep. Got up and took a walk. I've just written a real lousy poem to Viv.
   It was a poem in English wishing for silence, solitude, oblivion, and the "infinite freedom of the roaring wood," where there is no strife for the sake of rhyming with life.
Before and after dinner, a letter to Viv. Mailed it on the way to the reading room. Lucky me.

September 14, 1946
This morning, letter from Greenmeadow.

The usual
11 Sep. 1946.

   Our beloved John,
      Delight dispelled the longing at the very approach of your lovely letter. Thank you, Old Man. Yes, "The Autumn storms are roaming." But they, too, are passing.
      Did you receive the postcard reply from the MP written in the house of Commons. It left me in the same envelope as the 'notes' on the laburnum. […], Newspaper reports would have us understand that measures have been taken to release the POWs. Ernie looked in here on Sunday. There is no one now to listen to the observations about the Moon from a higher Level! My efforts on the roof yesterday are not quite satisfactory so another attempt will be made to-day, that is, if the weather will allow of such an ascent! The weather is certainly ruinous to the farmers! Our near neighbour hauled his wheat home the day it was reaped which is an unusual way to do. But in this way he saved it. The field I refer to is the one beyond the black gate where friends coming and going have collected a good deal of moisture! Our supply of coal is diminishing so presently–now 8.45–I shall be off yonder with my buckets. "Dilly" curious to know what I am doing has just leaped up onto my lap. Please write again soon.

Your affectionate Uncle William

Too wet today to attend Council Meeting. Auntie M. sends love and says she will write you again.

William

Waiting for answer from Viv.

September 16, 1946

Since last night, the mood has lifted and a marvelous confidence fills us. Tomorrow we could be transferred to Camp 409, supposedly the shipping camp. If it were only true! Actually I was lucky, since not everybody left. Since morning, letter to Viv and after the frisking last night, I met that friendly driver again, who always mailed my letters. Now I am sure that Ernie, too, will get my letter and that Viv will hear of my departure and now I am only waiting for tomorrow.

CAMP 409, WOLTERTON PARK, AYLSHAM

September 17, 1946

This morning we left 186. Train ride–Ipswich–Stow Market–Norfolk–Aylsham, near Cromer. Now we landed here after a six mile march. Fortunately only with hand luggage. This Camp 409 is supposed to be our last stop. The conditions here, however, allow very different conclusions. The huts stand in a gloomy forest; it was raining tonight, and the ground is muddy. The huts are like robbers' dens, dark, dirty, and dusty. Little food. Only to get away from here soon. When will it end, this going from place to place.

September 18, 1946

Food rather meagre. This morning Franz and I bound some twigs into a broom, and now it looks much better in the hut, somewhat cosy even. Above all we have three light bulbs. One could hardly see before. And somebody even made a fire in the stove. This morning suddenly I came across Max Kranzmeyer who was with me in the Austrian camp. He had been the fellow who had felt protected by Jesus when the bullets whizzed overhead.

September 19, 1946

I put on my marvellous overcoat and here I am sitting in the dining room with the Golden Treasury. *It's too cold for a walk; the air in the woods is too sharp, but also has a nice scent to it and, mixed with the wood smoke, reminds me of camping.*

September 20, 1946

Fade far away, dissolve and quite forget

> *What thou among the leaves hast never known,*
> *The weariness, the fever, and the fret,*
> *Here, where men sit and hear each other groan.*
> *Where palsy shakes a few, sad, last grey hairs,*
> *Where youth grows pale and spectre-thin and dies*
> *Where but to think is to be full of sorrow and leaden-eyed despair*
> *Where beauty cannot keep her lustrous eyes*
> *Or new love pine at them beyond tomorrow.*
> Keats.

These lines I found today in the Golden Treasury *and find them very appropriate for our situation. Not really. I'm lying on my bed after dinner, the fire is crackling. Everybody is asleep. The radio plays sentimental English music and it's almost cosy. On the next page in* The Golden Treasury, *I found some very beautiful words by the same poet which remind me of the 24th of June and I'm going to learn them by heart. In her last letter, Viv wrote about the poem by Keats and I think this is the one she meant:*

> *To one who has been long in city pent*
> *'Tis very sweet to look into the fair*
>
> *And open face of heaven, –to breathe a prayer*
> *Full in the smile of the blue firmament*
>
> *He mourns that day so soon has glided by*
> *Like the passage of an angel's tear*
> *That falls through the clear ether silently.*

And so it happened that I could forget and could get away from the first poem.

September 21, 1946

Last night powerful storm. This morning the rays of the sun fall through the trees and make our camp look friendlier at once. The dirty puddles are covered with leaves. The POWs are collecting wood and somebody is cutting wood in front of our huts. The air is so wonderfully fresh and scented and invites to a walk through the "park." We just picked three canteens full of mulberries which we keep in the huts for nibbling. Just memorized the second of the Keats poems.

September 29, 1946

The last few days the weather has been marvellous, and today too I spent the afternoon with Franz on the lawn. Even the food has become better and, through the help of the suns rays, we are free of hunger. But the nicest thing is that, according to the Tommy, our preparations are to be finished this coming Thursday, and so we can count on a departure soon. I hope that this time we really are in a shipping camp. My underwear is clean and, as far as I'm concerned, we could go tonight, but I'm afraid I'm going to finish my two years of captivity here in England. At the, moment, I'm reading a very interesting book by Alex Campbell, It's Your Empire (Left Book Club Edition.) It is not yet for public consumption, and, in general, it agrees with what that Swiss has explained to me. Once I am home, I'll ask him to send me a copy.

September 30, 1946
Yesterday we had to get out for roll call at 11:30 p.m. because somebody had crawled out through the barbed wire again. This happens here very often, since it has been proven that sugar beets, apples, and other green stuff will help conquer hunger. Actually, it isn't all that bad anymore, even if the soups are rather thin and their water content seems to approach that of the food in the concentration camps. They also changed the kitchen personnel.

Did I write this? Is this what people around me were saying? So somebody must have talked about the concentration camps. But my only mention of them was to complain of our food. Had I repressed those films so completely?

October 1, 1946
Two years a POW. This morning suddenly some names were read out, the others had to remain standing, and the ones whose names had been read were accompanied to the huts by sentries and they had to pack their things. Even the whole camp was surrounded by sentries. Kraemer Max was one of those. Apparently, he couldn't keep his mouth shut. The general idea is that they'll be sent to a black work camp. Actually, one isn't safe until one is at home and not even then, if you live in the British zone.

October 6, 1946
It has become rather chilly now and the first messengers of the autumn storms are chasing the leaves off the tall oak trees. At night, pygmy owls are howling and are haunting the dark like ghosts. Again, they make us wait another week. One can hardly believe anything anymore, and we hope to be at home at least by Christmas. But still, we allowed ourselves to be taken in by the words of the commanders, and hope for next week. I'm copying some sections from the book about the empire, and I'm translating an article into English which I will send to Viv for correction.

October 10, 1946
Letter to Viv.

October 14, 1946
Card to Mother. Last night I heard on the radio about a celebration in the banqueting hall

in Klosterneuburg. Anton Bruckner. Still no prospect of repatriation. We can only hope to be at home at Christmas. Am reading a beautiful book by Sinclair Lewis, Arrowsmith. A story of a doctor which Mother would like. Waiting for an answer from Viv. Something must come this week.

October 17, 1946

Today I finally dyed my Tommy coat. It is still in very good shape and will serve me well at home. Now it's drying in front of the barracks, and seems to glow with its awful lilac colour. It was the leads of indelible pencils which did the trick, and I just hope it won't rain when I'm wearing it, or I might be standing in a purple puddle. But never mind the colour, it's good material! Before lunch, letter from Greenmeadow. Answer to my POW card from the 1st. Long letter from Auntie. She writes as if I had left only yesterday, and how far back it all seems to me now. Something must come soon from Viv. Somewhat better mood because of the rumour that we are to leave on the 26th of October. Mother also wrote to Greenmeadow.

October 19, 1946

Franz just told me about the two islands in the Bristol Channel where he had worked for a few weeks. One of them I could see from Ruperra Castle quite well. I'd like to note down something about it since I really intend to come back to England again, and then it would be very nice to see those lonely places, especially since they're uninhabited and for sale. Maybe, one day, I could get through France to England by bike. Although Franz is thirty years old, he would be the right chum for such a trip. There certainly are many islands on the Welsh coast where one could live a marvellous hermit's life. Even if an island with cypresses in the Mediterranean would be more picturesque. Yes, I am dreaming, but these dreams will come true one day, I know it. I will go out again, on and on beyond the horizon. For a start here are two islands: Steep Holm–for sale. Empty buildings, seagulls, and other shore birds. No rats. A wall one to one-and-a-half kilometres long. 10 miles from Cardiff. Steep cliffs. The other one: Flat Holm, lighthouse, foghorn, library, empty hotel, rats. 7 miles from Cardiff. Barry.

October 21, 1946

A few days ago, I bought an American Botany book in exchange for my last cigarettes. It is full of marvellous photos and simply written. In the first chapter, they talk about two philosophies, vitalism and mechanism. The first reminds me of Gerhardt. I also discussed this with Franz and thought about it, but couldn't decide for either one. Is it not the one force that works in the simple laws of the atoms and in the highest stages of development in life? Is it not possible that human beings, in the progress of billions of years, will be able to develop their spiritual faculties perhaps by gaining new senses. Perhaps the secret of life is a *rose hidden behind numberless walls whose scent we are aware of but which we cannot see. Would it be possible for man, ever, to succeed in breaking through those walls and to face that rose one day. But wouldn't then the question still remain, who planted it? I come to no conclusion. we feel the original power in us, the power which the scientists hasten to discover without ever getting ever nearer to it. Aren't we closest to it when we let its powerful influence exert itself on us, and if we simply live life? I'm thinking of Rilke's* Book of Hours:

> *Du Dunkelheit, aus der ich stamme,*   *You darkness, of whom I am born—*
> *Ich liebe dich mehr als die Flamme,*   *I love you more than the flame*
> *Welche die Welt begrenzt,*   *that limits the world*
> *Indem sie glänzt*   *to the circle it illumines*
> *Für irgendeinen Kreis,...*   *and excluded all the rest.*
> *Aus dem heraus kein Wesen von ihr weiss.*

The darkness out of which life comes and to which we return, and which we all try to penetrate, everyone in his own way. Some may be explained mechanically by mutation and yet nobody knows the power which speaks in them and whom they serve.

> *Geheimnisvoll am lichten Tag*
> *Mysterious in bright daylight, never*
> *Läßt sich Natur des Schleiers nicht berauben.*
> *Will nature be defrauded of her veil.*
> (Goethe)

And yet our searching always leads to more and more amazement. Now I also understand Arrowsmith's prayer: God give me strength not to trust in God. The prayer of the scientist who is not satisfied with the existence of a primeval power, but who wants to recognize it. With the help of it, they, the leaders of reason, together with the leaders of feeling, are the true priests of humanity. Both feel eternity in them. I don't come to any end.

Letter from Viv:

Newport, Mon.
October 1946

Dear Horst,

    I was most surprised to discover that you are still here in this country. When your Uncle handed me the official card you had sent, I could hardly believe my eyes. I had thought that you were in Vienna and had vividly imagined you at home with your Mother. I had written to you there and was patiently awaiting a reply giving me a full and glowing account of your return home and all its happiness. But Horst, how very fortunate though, to find that you are near Norwich, for I shall be visiting relatives at Tibbenham, a little village not far from Norwich, on the 25th October and staying with them until November 4th. There is just a chance that you will still be there, though I would wish much, much more, you will have started on the outward journey long before then. Though I do not know whether I shall be permitted to visit you, yet it seems too golden an opportunity to miss and so I am writing the officer in charge to ask whether such a visit can be arranged. So great is the joy at the prospect of returning home and so unbounding the enthusiasm to be off that one is apt to forget the thousands of others who have to be repatriated, too. Your turn will come, that is certain. I hope and pray it will be soon, very, very soon. [...]. Yesterday at Greenmeadow while we were having tea, one dear wish was expressed by the three of us. I was hoping that the day would be bright and warm in the sunshine, for I longed to see the Channel once more from the little hill. But no, it was cold, grey and wintry and the view was cloudy. Yet, when I closed my eyes, I could see and feel the sunshine and lived again the happy moments of another day. A brown bracken has taken the place of the wavy grass. The field of oats is now one of grass, and the flowers have faded from the garden. Winter is a little sad. Horst, it is the coldness without the sun that I do not like. The parcels I tried to send your Mother have been returned to me and the postage refunded. I have not the heart to open them. Would that I could send them her. Maybe soon the ban will be lifted. I have written this to Camp 409 thinking that it is possible that you are still there and longing for a letter from us with a little news.

All my love, Viv

October 22, 1946
Finally, something seems to happen. Today our names were read according to the zones to which we are going to be released. For me that will be the American zone so that I can see

(Opposite page and this one) Envelopes of Letters Sent to Horst While Waiting to Be Repatriated in Various Camps in England

my sister first before going on to Vienna. I'm so curious about how things are going to turn out. Will I feel like a stranger? If I only were there already. Outside in the park the trees are in the yellow of autumn, and leaves are constantly falling. I hope nature won't be too dreary when we come home. But I must be crazy! Just to be home and finally to be resting in freedom! How nice it will be to spend the winter evenings with Mother and not to have crowds around me! And Ilse! Has she changed? When will we see each other for the first time? It can only be another week before we get out of here. Yes, my thoughts are at home in my room, on the slopes of the Vienna woods; skiing up on the hill with Ilse. Yes, you must have met many friends. It has been nearly three years, but I do know that you are fond of me. However, I'm thinking back of that evening when we were fighting about certain words in the Iphigenia *and how something broke in me that moment, but we found each other again. Your dear tender words you wrote to me in the POW camps, and which made me so happy, seem to come straight from your heart that never opened itself to me so much before. How I am looking forward to seeing you again to hold your hands again and to feel your friendship. Yes, and I realize that this friendship will last. Are you expecting a Horst that has grown up or will you be disappointed after having met so many "mature" people at the university? Disappointed to find a Horst as inexperienced as he was when he left you. But he has become harder, and I'm glad to know that. Perhaps more used to doing without and going his own way. And yet, were you not always with me and will not everything be forgotten and everything drown in the first kiss? I'm dreaming myself into this dream when I lie in bed or when I walk outside, and the dry leaves are rustling as I walk. But I wake up again, and it is painful to wake up again into a sceptical reality, the hard thorny shield against disappointments…But wait, am I not young? Isn't the whole world open to me! And I do believe in friendship.*

Among the letters I find one of the few Auntie Mary wrote to me. In her very own way she brought Greenmeadow near to me once more before it would swept away by the excitement of leaving the island. I discovered late that she was as fond of quoting as Uncle, and how much the quotes characterized each of them. Mary, too, wrote with a quill, as far as I can make out.

GreenMeadow
Llanfedwy
Oct. 15/46

Dear John,

I had a beautiful letter from your mother. She was well, but very lonely. She is anxiously awaiting the return of her son which I sincerely hope will not be long, and before the very short days come. Viv came along on Saturday, and spent most of the day here. She went for a walk up the 'hill'. It was a lovely day, and she enjoyed it very much. She stayed until about 8 oc., then she intended going to meet a bus at Castleton which is about 4 miles from here. She is a fine walker, and I believe that is why she keeps so fit. [...]. Ernie was here a week last Saturday, still very busy, and working late.

I hope you are able to continue with your studies. We shall picture you indulging in your favourite winter sports shortly. We have some grand old mountains in Wales too. For instance the Breconshire Beacons, where the little wild ponies graze, and also the lesser hills. There are beautiful bits of country scenery around these parts, and I believe the oaks and beech trees cannot be beaten. Presently I am going my favourite part of the road, to post the letters-the road runs by Ruperra Park wall, with an avenue of trees inside; I mean the park side. There is no-one at the Castle now except the caretakers. Well–John be a good boy, do as you are asked to do, and all will be well. Have faith and courage a little longer,

> A faith that shines more clear and bright
>   When tempests rage without.
> That when in danger knows no fear,
>   In darkness knows no doubt.

Would it not be grand if we all had such faith as that?

When you are free again do go out in the world, remember always to lead a clean life–lend a helping hand to those in need, be kind to all dumb animals, and do nothing that is unmanly. Think of the lines:

> "I dare do all that may become a man;
> Who dares do more is none."

Do not think I'm preaching at you, John. It is because I have your welfare at heart that I speak thus. The table is now laid for tea. Blackberry and apple tart and *Welsh* cakes. "So we will go to our places..." to be continued.

With best wishes and affection, from Aunty

Dinky and Dilly are well–Dilly goes up onto the roof with Uncle and sometimes she sits on the coping. We have not been able to secure the services of a plasterer as yet. So Uncle is doing his best to repair as much as he himself can.

October 23, 1946
Finally we have a repatriation roll call. Our clothes were checked. Today it was officially announced: British Zone, Friday, American and French Zone, Sunday, Russian and Vienna, Tuesday. So another four days, at last.

October 25, 1946
To my greatest joy and surprise, I got two letters from Viv a few minutes ago. One of the thirteenth of October. The damn laziness in the interpreter's office where it was lying so long. Viv wanted to visit me. Today, on the 25th, she arrived at her relatives in Norwich. Her request for a visit was rejected. From the second letter I could see that my letter of the 10th of August had not reached Newport. I'm so mad at myself that I trusted that doctor. Yes, it's not everybody's business to keep one's word. Damn doctors. But I was still very happy with the letter.

It was the very last one I received from her or from Uncle in a POW camp–a last send-off into freedom:

Newport, Mon.
October 20th 1946

Dear Horst,

I am sorry I must write to tell you I cannot be allowed to see you. I had wanted to so very much but only visits from the nearest relations concerned can be considered. But what a near relationship friendship can be! There is something so final, "inhuman" about regulations that one is left stranded, conscious only of a feeling of having been condemned without a trial. No. I am not complaining; regulations there must be. It can never be given to anyone to understand what our friendship is. Only we ourselves can know.

So much was my longing to see you that last Thursday night my thoughts of you awakened me. I was aware of the docks and ships, vague and shadowy, in the cold, grey, misty light of dawn, and you bidding us goodbye. As I watched the scene, I was made glad and happy. But almost immediately the mind of me intervened with, "This is merely wishful thinking. You cannot go to see Horst, and so you desire that already he is sailing away to Austria, for that would lessen your disappointment." Maybe so. I know much as I long to hear of your return, I shall not believe it until your letter arrives from Austria bearing the certain news. And so until then, I shall continue to write this one-sided correspondence. ...

I will not write more this time for I want to enclose a poem of Keats that I think you will like and a few quotations of Browning's which I have found to be a constant source of aspiration when life has been uncertain and the future grey.

I'm always close to you in my thinking. All my love, Horst,

yours affectionately,

Viv

[The poem by Keats was "I stood tip-toe upon a little hill"]

PS I like Browning because of his great strength and optimism. His thought I often find too deep and involved. But the bits I've written have been of great help to me.

[Enclosed were four Browning quotes.]

Goodbye England! The day after tomorrow, I'm getting out of here and soon I can write to Viv without any restrictions. Viv wrote about Mother, that she is waiting, longingly. Yes, I'll be soon with you. Tonight all those who go to the British Zone left, and on Sunday it's our turn, and then on to Dover and off this island.... Franz is leaving me tonight.

October 27, 1946
Our luggage is already at the station and we're waiting to march there tonight at 8. By now Franz is surely on the continent already and maybe we'll be on French soil tomorrow morning. We finally made it, at last. 7 p.m. A storm is whipping through the Park, and yellow leaves are tossing in the wind. Soon we will be marching...

October 28, 1946
Left the station at twenty minutes after midnight.
On the train.

Survived the march pretty well. Spent the night more or less comfortably on the train by resting my head on the little table. In the dawn we pass the suburbs of London eastward to the Downs. We just passed hop plantations.

9:20 Finally on board. The cliffs of Dover have disappeared and nothing but water all around. It's really rocking now.

12:30 central European time. Transit camp Calais. There will be some food immediately. I'm mad at myself because, during the last ten minutes of the crossing, I had to give my offering to Neptune. Well, there's a first time for everything. Brisk wind in the harbor. Dirty French kids, demolished bunkers, German POWs.

Later: Now I have some time to write about my goodbye to England in more detail. At Aylsham station we waited for an hour before our train was shunted to the platform. In the dawn the shadows of suburban houses moved by. We crossed the Thames, and the train took us East where morning was glowing between the clouds.

Maidstone-Ashford. I'm sitting among unknown "comrades". I like it better that way than to have to stare into faces I know. Folkestone appears with the first chalk cliffs, and now the sea beckons in a golden sheen between the dunes. On the left, the cliffs, glowing white—in only a few more minutes we finally reach Dover at 9:15. We're being handed over to a different officer, counted, and a few minutes later we're sitting on a slightly rocking ferry boat. And off we go between two piers; we're leaving the harbor. Through a porthole I'm watching the gentle whitecaps and the gulls rushing down into them. Behind us the white cliffs are gleaming below a dim autumn sky. The pale sun is shining on the green sea. England, goodbye. I'm thinking of Viv, of the last letter and how fast everything happened. Soon the waves are rising and the boat begins to toss, and I go back to my seat. Now and then a pale swaying figure gropes for the railing. A British soldier sitting near me vomits into his helmet which has the perfect shape for that purpose, and the sour smell gets to me, too. I have to give in, and am mad at myself because right now the loudspeaker says "Get ready to disembark." The English vacationers are leaving the boat, and we follow them. The cold sea air refreshes me, and everything is forgotten. Here we are. We stand on the continent. The moment we have been waiting for two years. A new leaf in our lives is turned. Yes, here was the war. From the terribly monotonous hills, the gun openings of crude concrete bunkers stare. Now and then, bullet marks. Rusty iron girders, camouflage nets in tatters. Dirty children with knees red from the cold are running around and come to meet us, and we march to the transit camp where we have to wait until 5 o'clock in the afternoon. Now and then, a ship's siren. In a few hours, we won't hear them anymore, and France will accept us.

29 October
Left Calais last night at 19:50. Lille at 22:00. This morning Chalons sur Marne.

Comfortable coaches, but unheated. The train is one for British soldiers on leave, going to Villach. I hope we can get off at Salzburg. 10 o'clock, I see Nancy again. To the east the Vosges. Beautiful German autumn forest. Tunnels. Strasbourg. At Kehl, we cross the Rhine River. French Occupation Zone. Kehl completely destroyed. Starving children wave up to our train. On top of the rail road huts, the French flag is flying. Everywhere German POWs with French sentries. Must be awful: in your own country. We go on to Rastatt, which is completely destroyed. In the fields, we see only women and old men harvesting turnips. They don't look well, but are friendly and wave to us. Now we stand in Karlsruhe. Just talked with a civilian. Upbeat mood. Waiting for food. So far we got one sixth of a can of corned beef and a few biscuits. In one hour, that is 17:30, we go on. What we've seen of our home country so far is quite depressing. We imagined our return more joyful and merrier. But that's not so easy with an empty stomach; we are tired and outside the window the ruins and the starving faces. How is it going to be at home?

Austria

October 30, 1946
Salzburg. We arrived this morning. Red Cross nurses. Coffee. Now we're waiting to see whether we can be discharged here or have to go on to Villach. Already some of us have friends and relatives coming to the train windows! People here look better than in Germany, even if they bitch about everything. Traces of the war can be seen here, but it's not so bad. I write a Red Cross card to Mother. It is a foggy morning, the sky is grey, and our joy rather subdued. If we could only get off the train here, I could be at Ruth's tonight. I can hardly believe it. Four days ago I was still behind barbed wire.
17:00. Discharge Camp Hallein. Americans all over. We still have to spend the night in these windowless huts. I hope I won't have any trouble because of where I really live, and I hope Ruth is in St. Gilgen. It's actually a little risky of me to go on like this, since it's not so easy to change zones. The mountains, already covered with snow, looking down at us, and on the slopes, the autumn trees glow. Not far from here, there's supposed to be a detention camp for some 1,000 Nazis.

Hallein, October 31
Still in the same camp. Today people for the American Zone are discharged. My papers have the Vienna address, and so I'm going to be discharged here but sent on to Vienna. I hope I can interrupt my journey so that I can see Ruth. Then my plan would have succeeded completely. I hope to get out of here soon and not to have to spend another cold night here. Before I leave the camp, they'll frisk me once more.

November 1, 1946 St. Gilgen.
Here I am, sitting in a fairy tale land with friendly fairies around me in the midst of a beautiful landscape! It worked out after all. I was discharged yesterday afternoon. In a few minutes, there I am, standing on the platform, a civilian. How different everything looks. And all by myself, I go to a little store and buy myself a roll and five dekagrams of sausage. And then, on the small-gage railroad, two hours to St. Gilgen. It is dark now, and I ask my way to Hotel Radetzky, but Ruth isn't there. But I am happy to know that she is somewhere in this town. A man with one leg is coming down the street, and I ask him about her. He has just been with Ruth and takes me to her. And then, the first moment. She has changed, has put on weight and speaks a rather heavy dialect, and everything is so strange. I imagine myself in a dream. Ruth is telling me about Mother, Klosterneuburg, Ilse. Now, as I'm writing this, I'm already used to Ruth, if only her friends were not here. The one with one leg is a locksmith from Vienna and a real tough, a poor devil who enjoys Ruth's pity. The married couple is awful and disgusting, and I wish nothing better than to be away from here. I'm just not at home yet. How nice it'll be to be home in the familiar surroundings, and Mother will certainly understand when I tell her that, for the time being, I don't want to see anybody, and that I would like it best to be in a mountain hut all by myself and look at the beautiful landscape greeting me with snow white peaks. This afternoon, a stroll with Ruth and the invalid. Of course, he had to be along. He has no tact at all, but the landscape is gorgeous and consoles me for everything. Up on the Weisswand, I buy a picture postcard and have just written one to Viv. Won't she be surprised! This morning, I sent a telegram to Mother. I was even at the barber and enjoyed the civilized service. It is really natural that, at the moment, I am so misanthropic, but I've got used to Ruth already. I'll still be glad when I'm in the train to Vienna and walk the old ways, and I'm very curious to see Ilse. It strikes me that Ruth seems to have become a teenager again, since her partner left her. Tomorrow morning, both of us will go up to an empty hut in the hills. I can hardly believe that I would choose such a lonely hut as a refuge, but at least I hope to be alone with Ruth tomorrow. To my joy, I found some English books at Ruth's place, and now we're going to have dinner at The Grape. Yes, there's plenty of food around here, and one would hardly notice that this is a zone of military occupation and that there has been a war here, if it were not for those crippled by the war.

November 2, 1946
Mother sent a package to Ruth, and she went to the Post Office to get it. So I am alone. I like to be alone and to have a few hours to myself. Outside, the quiet lake; I hear its gentle waves against the shore. Through the autumn fog, dimly, the colours of the trees on the other shore beckon. Here in the room it smells of comfortable warmth. The longer I am alone with Ruth the more I'm getting used to her, and the closer I get to my sister again.

Even her acquaintances bother me less now. And the people she works with are nicer than the others, and even the lady with whom we had to eat lunch struck me as not too bad, but I'm longing for quiet and I'm looking so forward to home. This morning, I bought a wooden plate with a scene burnt into it as a Christmas present for Viv. Will she be surprised! It's so cosy here. Sheep Mountain is glowing red in the sunshine and luring me with its snowy glory. I must go skiing this winter.

November 3, 1946
Last night Franz was here again, whom I don't like, and who disturbed our peace. Last night we went to the movies because Ruth likes that so much, and we saw a sentimental American film about heroes. The film ripped several times and finally, at 11, it was all over. Today, it was even more beautiful. Even if we had to sit together with Mrs. So and So. But, in the afternoon, we were alone again and, in glorious weather, we went up the first of the "Three Brothers" and looked at the empty cabin. After that, we went along the lake on the general path. Tonight we eat at home and we're rather tired. I'm not used to anything anymore. My kit bag is packed again and tomorrow Ruth is coming with me to Salzburg, and I'll try to get to Vienna as soon as possible. It's like coming back from leave, but now I can stay at home. I still cannot imagine it, and sometimes I'm afraid something could still happen.

November 5, 1946
This afternoon with Ruth in Salzburg; we spent some happy hours together. We went window shopping, bought a few things, and walked through the narrow streets. We even found the house in which Paracelsus lived. There was a light drizzle as we went through the narrow streets, our arms linked. Salzburg is such a neat town. Now I am alone again, and I no longer miss Ruth. I'm going to Klosterneuburg and she won't be there. She came to the station with me, and then she went to the movies by herself to see an awful English movie. At 22:46, passenger train to this place: Attnang Puchheim. I'm sitting on my kitbag and wait til it's 3:30; that's when a freight train is going to Linz, and I might be able to catch the fast train to Vienna from there. It is too good to be true. But I'm happy no matter what. How's it going to be in the Russian Zone?

November 5, 1946 Linz.
The freight train was ok, and I can be in Linz an hour and a half before the fast train to Vienna. Now I sit here and let the Austrian Red Cross take care of me, and wait for tomorrow morning, 7:00. In the afternoon, I even have to go through the delousing station. Before that, I must get the pass to cross the zone. What a run-around. I hope I won't get it all over again at home. This morning in the drizzly rain I took a walk through the town. An unfriendly, almost hopeless dump. Just to get away from here. My consolation is that

tomorrow morning, at this time, I'll be on the moving train.
3:00 p.m. Now I finally got my pass and the permit to use the fast train. Roll on tomorrow morning...

The first deep breath of freedom I had taken in St. Gilgen; I had walked where I wanted, nobody stopped me, no barbed wire. I was with Ruth, almost at home simply by being with her, though the surroundings were still strange. A kind of second thrust into freedom I felt on that freight train. It brought back dreary memories of army transports, but, not being a soldier any more, I felt as happy as a hobo. On the passenger train to Vienna I advanced (?) to the state of a free citizen returning from the Salzburg Lake District. My homecoming was not a total surprise. I did not drop out of the sky. Every day the radio announced the names of POWs to be discharged.

Mother did not have a radio but Ilse would race to her on her bike to call out: "Der Horst kommt!" ("Horst is coming!"). I had not been able to let them know on which train I would arrive, and nobody was at the West Station to meet me. I took the tram to the local train. In an hour I would be home, home!

November 6 was a cold damp day, and I wore my purple, "cardinal's" coat as I walked up the hill, gave our family whistle, and ran past the kitchen window to the back door. And there was Mother. I don't remember what we said or did that day. All I remember is the joy, and I can still feel it today.

Looking back over the two years as a POW it has become clear to me that the year at the bakery at Ruperra stands out as a time of peaceful work after and before the often frustrating waiting time as a useless number in a crowd of numbers. The few weeks of Greenmeadow were so much more than that. Those weeks stood out as a haven of human kindness, warmth, and innocence that took on a spiritual quality that I may not have been fully aware of at the time, but which has grown in the years since.

Where was Wales now? Far, far behind me. Worlds away. Not quite. It was waiting for me right there on my table at home. In her letter of Oct. 13 Viv had mentioned that she had written a letter to Vienna thinking that I would be home already. Now I had finally caught up with it. Like all her letters it was brimming with exuberance, willingness to help, and a trust in my abilities. How could I ever live up to the expectations of such a friend and teacher?

Newport, Mon.
Sunday, Sept. 23, 1946

Dear Horst

How does it feel at home in Vienna? I can imagine the wild joy of your freedom. Can you really believe that it has happened? On your first enthusiasm take care you do not overdo it. I am strongly hoping that you will begin the October term at the University. I shall follow your University career with great interest and I hope to share it a little. Horst, may there be a straight steady rising to the summit for you. Do not forget that any help that I can give you is yours unreservedly. Our friendship is an assurance of that. Books I can send you, and any help my poor brain is capable of giving you is yours too. How I look forward to your next visit to Wales. It will be our turn for great rejoicing then! How soon, I wonder, will they permit me to travel as far as Vienna? I suppose you are about 40 hours away. Not far really—Is it? Your freedom brings our meeting nearer. How glad I am to feel that the confining prison days are over. I only watch for a letter from you now bearing the Vienna postmark; then I shall know that all is well. I send this to you with all my joy and hope that a bright and happy future is in store for you.

All my love, Viv

Uncle William's last letter to me at a POW camp had been returned to him with the stamp "Addressee Repatriated;" he had sent it on to Austria.

Greenmeadow, Llanfedwy, St. Melan's,
Cardiff
Michaelmas Day 1946

Our beloved John,

Dear old Dame Nature has been weeping for our misdeeds! The trickling streamlet has become a mighty watercourse, and all the innumerable, falling tears, swelling the normal flow, have been hastening on down to the deep! Where is there one among us willing to admit that our small ways do not dovetail into the Great Eternal Plan! The tearful clouds have been shedding off their abundance through day and through night, and the prospect has become very serious. These lead-coloured clouds remind me of a picture that was exhibited in Cardiff, some fifty years ago. Wind borne clouds, broken and almost black, all over, and huge rolling breakers, making for the shore. By Mr. Fussell of Anvioth Castle, and his title of it "The Promise of a Wild Night." How are you keeping? V. was here on Saturday and brought with her some very acceptable literature which we read with eagerness. Ernie, too, on Sunday produced, just after his arrival here, a letter which he received from a friend. Thank you, John, for your kindly reference to us, as you know we would have you be near us always, but there are certain times of the day when this silent wish finds vocal expression. Can you guess the times of day I am alluding to? Of course, you can. Apples have now succeeded gooseberries in our daily menu.

Adverting to an expression in one of your dear letters—"How little men and history have changed." It came to my mind yesterday as I was transporting some coal from the spot where it was dropped some weeks ago; the motive power in removing this combustible is the same as it was during the building of the pyramids!! The speeding gale we have just experienced tore away some fairly big branches from our oak trees, uprooted an apple tree, and left others in a very humble position. Yes, "The autumn storms are roaming!"

This letter was started a few days ago, but circumstances caused me to postpone further writing then, and this afternoon, no sooner had the pen been dipped in the ink when Ernie called. Ernie has departed and the quill is in action again! V. was here yesterday and climbed the heights! It was almost dark when she left here for the bus at 8:00 p.m. The "longing" has got hold of us again. Wind from the East today: bright sunshine during the morning but this afternoon it got quite dark just as though the sun was eclipsed. The dear little brown squirrel has come around

> "The Verdant Pastures".
> Surrounded by beautiful trees.
> Your Home in Wales.
>
> Our beloved John,—
>
> The gentle breezes have borne away the obscuring cloud and, thankful we are that you are homeward bound! We trust that you will find your dear mother and sister and all old friends quite well. How delighted they will all be at the re-union. We always feel that you are near us, more so, when we are perusing your lovely letters, which we do as often as we can. Your touching lines have found a deep, and an abiding place in our hearts. Yes, old man, true are the words — "Even this shall pass away", and, equally true is the fact that the disturbing effects of the memorable 26th of June still linger in their fulfilment! The little we were able to do for you could not possibly compensate for the pleasure your companionship gave us. We were to you a "spark in the night". You were to us a bright and shining

From a Letter "Uncle William" Sent to Horst Back in Austria with Censorship Stamp

> John
> Philosophy
> air before wear garments
> uncle.

"Uncle William's" Typical Cautionary Advise Attached to His Letter

again. The top of the big gate at the back served as a bridge for it to get across the gateway.

  All our best love from

    Auntie and your affectionate Uncle William

"How does it feel at home?" Viv had asked long before I was even there. Now, so many years later, how can I recapture that feeling? I did not keep a journal in those days. Writing down my emotions would have changed them, reduced them. Now I can only "think" my way back.

I had been away for three years. The first of these was in the army; I was home several times on leave, and being there was always overshadowed by having to go away again soon. I remember one of those "good byes" on a grey morning at the train station. Mother had always held back her tears. This time, when I turned around for a last look, her face was contorted by suffering; she wept as I had never seen her weep before. She turned her face to the wall, and stepped back into the dark doorway. After the war she told me that an old man who had been passing by had said to her: "He'll come back!"

Now I was back, for good. Mother's one wish during all those three long years was fulfilled. She was happy, well, and looked it. She was fifty seven, but there was no trace of grey in her rich black hair. There was none of that worry, that devastated expression in the photo on her identity card when she had been waiting for her two children whom the war had taken so far away. Throughout the uncertainty, the misery and terror of war, a second war for her, she had remained herself. For me she was unchanged.

As I entered my room the three years vanished. But everything was familiar and strange at the same time; strange because time seemed to have stood still. I was in the museum of my boyhood. There was my table, the gaudy print of the mountain range above it, and below it on the wall the pennant from the Grossglockner alpine highway, a souvenir from the bike trip that I had taken all alone that last summer of 1943. There was grandfather's wardrobe, too big for the few books, the fewer clothes. There was my bed by the window: sitting up I used to see the sunrise through the branches of the pear tree. My very own den was unchanged. The house was unchanged except for my favourite reading place, the glassed-in veranda under the huge walnut; in stormy weather its branches would knock against the windows. On clear days I would look up from my book and see the valley below me and the yonder slope that stretched to the horizon. Now, not one pane was whole, the windows were boarded up. That brought me back to the present and the war. But we had been fortunate.

The losses were insignificant. After the fighting, Russian soldiers had gone looting from house to house, willful like children not knowing what to take and what to leave or throw away. There wasn't much to take in our little house up on the hill. Maybe it was out of disappointment that they had scattered my stamp collection in the garden, and mother had to salvage what the wind had not blown away. They had taken my concertina and left me a tennis racket they had picked up somewhere else on their jaunt. And, as mother had reported to me in Ruperra, they had taken my sling shot and that old rusty relic of a six-shooter that hadn't even worked with caps. But the urn that held grandfather's ashes they had not touched. Mother had not been home when they came; in those critical days the women of the neighbourhood would stay together, and later, when things had quieted down, Mother's rusty Czech could mediate occasionally when a Russian soldier would bring a brick of margarine and ask the woman of the house to fry him a mess of potatoes just the way he wanted them.

One dark night, Mother was back in the house again, alone as always, when somebody tried to get in through the kitchen window which was low to the ground. But the double windows resisted, glass splintered. Mother, in her bed in the adjoining room, quickly slipped into my heavy ski-boots and stomped around the room with heavy tread imitating the sound of a man in the house. The visitor quickly took off. She opened her window, shouted "Achtung, Achtung, Dieb!" ("Watch out! Watch out! Thief!"), and threw a heavy wooden bowl onto the neighbour's roof to alert them. Later the neighbours established a warning system with referee whistles.

Such were the first stories I heard. Mother told them with her own ironic sense of humour. Perhaps she did not want to break our happy mood with darker truths. But day by day I heard other stories that put a bitter edge on idyllic memories. Down by the brook where we had played soccer the Russians had shot a writer in whose house they had found a hunting gun. And there was the terror under Nazi rule: A local girl who had slept with a Polish POW had her head shaved and had to watch as her lover was hanged on the hill on a meadow where we used to go with Mother on a Sunday afternoon to pick flowers. That, too was "home"; not the home I had been longing for in my romantic verse. When the Russians had entered Klosterneuburg mother had been with many others in the deep cellars of the Abbey which promised sanctuary—the scenes she witnessed there! Mothers on their knees begging for mercy, in despair over their raped daughters, the Russian officer saying in perfect German: "Now you are crying, not so long ago our mothers were crying." That was the other side of the story which so many Austrians, all "victims," forgot when they told me what they had been through.

When I came home nobody talked about the concentration camps. Only later I read Victor E. Frankl's lectures about his survival in Buchenwald: ... *trotzdem ja zum Leben sagen. (1947)* (...*To say yes to life in spite of it*), and Eugen Kogon's *Der SS-Staat. Das System der deutschen Konzentra-tionslager.* (1947)(*The Theory and Practice of Hell*) Those pictures of Bergen-Belsen that I had seen in Chepstow came back in my memory and my conscience. Uncle William's question about German atrocities was finally answered; I had to believe what I had thought impossible, unthinkable. I tried to answer, for myself, Kogon's question of how much ordinary people knew. I am sure that I did not know what was going on in the camps. But from what I know now I must have at least heard of things that should have demanded my questions. And I don't know what I as a teenager would have, could have done had I known the truth. When I did know it the question of the conscious or unconscious involvement of my generation began to haunt me.

Now, far removed from my sheltered life in Wales, I had to face the knowledge of two kinds of brutality: the brutality done *by* "my people," the horror of the death camps, the calculated evil, "which nothing at all in the power of man can ever clean again" (Primo Levi), and the brutality done *to* "my people," the actions of Russian soldiers in 1945 that I heard too much about; they were "explainable" as acts of war, a war that did not stop the mass murder of millions in the camps but ended a tyranny.

There was a Russian garrison in my home town and a Russian Kommandatura in a side street, and we avoided walking by there. On the crowded bus to Vienna, I would often stand next to one of the a heavily perfumed Russian officers with their wide pink or purple shoulder pieces. When I came home late in 1946 the first wave of soldiers who had taken the town in May 1945 had long been replaced by young troops: draftees, they looked like to me. After manoeuvres, they marched through our streets: blond farm boys in their belted khaki tunics, reeking of sweat and leather, roaring their songs that sounded barbaric because we didn't understand a word. We must have looked and sounded very much like them when we marched through Czech towns.

Being home again, I had to face my past in the German army, how I, giving in to peer pressure, ideas of manliness, and propaganda, had been eager to defend a fatherland that wasn't even mine; Hitler had made Austria a part of Germany, and too many Austrians had been willing to be swallowed up. My only consolation was that my personal "action" in that defence had been no action at all: my two shots in the air had not killed anybody. But I had been a willing part of the war machine. Our eyes had been kept on the enemy without.

My home-coming, connecting to past and present, happened in stages and on different levels. Mother and Ilse, the two persons who at the time meant most to me, were there. They were my anchor as I drifted between past and future. Some of my class mates were scattered all over Austria and maybe beyond, I didn't know. A few I met at the funeral of my favourite Latin teacher who had died of kidney failure, supposedly after blows with a rifle butt when he was taken prisoner. My French teacher, and the English teacher to whom I had written from a POW Camp, had panicked when the Russians approached, and shot themselves. The past had broken into splinters: nostalgia, mass deception, self deception, happy memories, false ambitions, naivete, ignorance, hope, illusion, disillusionment, terrible decisions I had been spared–every time I turned the kaleidoscope the splinters scattered and fell into a new confusion. It would take time to steady it into some meaningful part of my life. I was twenty one, and it was time to at least to be aware of the puzzle, the questions. True answers would have to wait. But the present was one grateful amazement at how lucky I had been and was. Greenmeadow was one reason for that amazement.

The letters from Wales came from another world, and I had been in that world while all the horror and suffering had happened where I now was. I needed the letters to prove that that other world actually did exist; and yet these letters were almost unreal to me. I was caught up in being home again after those three years, and in the feeling that life was before me, that things could only get better. I lived with Mother in the three-room house which she had been renting since the 1930s. The one cold-water faucet was in the cellar. But post-war reconstruction had given us electricity, for lighting only, however. Mother was again working in the same clothing factory where she had worked before and during the war, again doing piece work, like hemming dress shields. She never bought a piece of clothing herself, and only wore things given to her by others. There was never a word, or even look of reproach about my being totally dependent upon her. If there was tension between us it arose whenever I, in love and thoughtless, had spent too many evening hours with Ilse. Mother was hurt; she would not go to sleep until she heard me come in no matter how quiet I tried to be. She wanted me to go to the university, and shared everything with me to make this possible. Never having had more than mere necessities, we did not find it hard to accept post-war realities. The few clothes I ever had could only have tempted the poorest of looters but they had disappeared. I wore the military jacket, unusual in its dark green colour and without a patch on the back, that I had selected as a perfect fit in the last repatriation camp. But it was getting colder every day; I had never had a winter coat. Now I did—the one some British officer had discarded and I had grabbed in Derby. But it had to be dyed again. The festive Cardinal's purple had to give way to a humble Capuchin dark brown, more appropriate to a modest student beginning his first semester.

On November 15, I registered at the University of Vienna. The fastest route to a job was to work for a teacher's diploma. You had to have two majors, and I chose German and English. I registered late and took many courses to get through as fast as possible. In German I took many classes with Ilse, but, in spite of that amorous incentive, I put my best energies into English. I felt superior to all those poor lambs who had not had the advantage of being POWs in Wales.

November 27, 1946

Our beloved John,

Your most welcome and anxiously expected letter of which we became possessed yesterday confirmed the indirect news it was our joy to peruse a few days before when Viv came along with her consolation prize! How lovely when you reached the old 'Home' to find your dear mother well, and the immediate and familiar surroundings unchanged—quite different to the experience of someone I read about long years ago—" All had changed except the melancholy cooing of the wood pigeon."

We were truly glad to hear that your daily hours are now spent among the learned professors. Please be on the look-out for a parcel of worn clothing which I understand we are allowed to send. Letter to follow. All our love to your dear mother and self.

Your affectionate Uncle and Auntie

What a difference between my teachers at Greenmeadow and those at the University in Vienna. The "learned professors" may have been learned but what did they profess in their impersonal mass feedings called lectures? They certainly lacked Viv's fervour.

Every letter from Uncle William and from Viv helped me hold on to Greenmeadow, that Happy Isle that threatened to drift away from me in time and space.

Uncle William's letters worked their charm in Austria perhaps even more than when I had read them in the repatriation camps. Then I had had his voice in my ear, somehow we shared the same language air. Now, in my German language world his letters, written with the quill, brought him with them like a dear visitor from a foreign continent. None of my English professors spoke his English, and he came to me only. Neither Mother nor Ilse could read English, and in translation Uncle William would lose like a good poem. He brought with him Greenmeadow, and he told of everyday life in Wales as only he could. From my lectures at the University of Vienna, I would never have known that Wales even existed.

Greenmeadow
November 29, 1946

...And now for some news nearer the present day–a few days before the 6th inst. We received a letter from Blanch, Aberdare, and another from Norah, Mountain Ash, informing us that their uncle Eddie—our cousin had departed into the realms of the unseen and would be buried on that day in Cardiff Cemetery, and that his body would rest over Wednesday night in the Church of Merthyr Vale– an edifice his three sisters—now departed—did so much by various means to erect. In order to attend the service up there I set out to meet an early bus from near Maenllwyd Inn near Rudry. This bus got into Caerphilly just in time for me to miss the train for the nearest station (Aberfan) to the Church. Having lost both bus and train I made known my position to a young gentleman, in the garb of a porter. Politely and diligently he traced for me on the suspended time table the times of departure from, and the times of

Identification Documents of Horst's Mother, Maria Anna Jarka, 1946

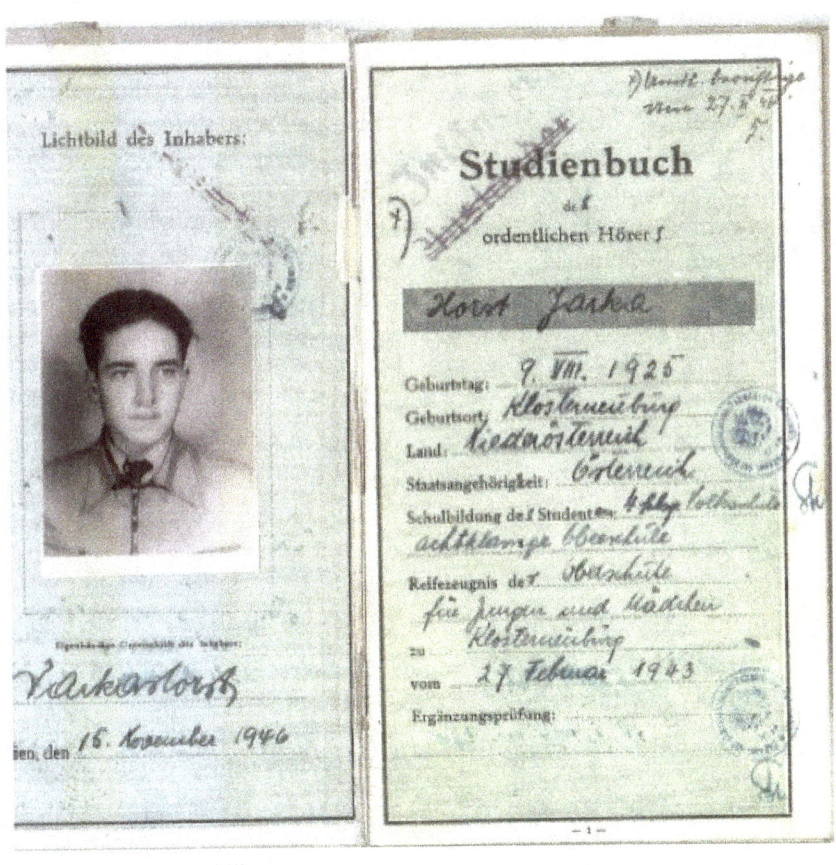

Horst's University of Vienna "Studienbuch," 15 November 1946

arrival at, the destination I wished to reach. It was better for me that I had missed the earlier train out. For his cheerful and ready assistance (without cringing) I have addressed a letter of praise to the Station Master referring to the incident. The train reached the end of my journey in good time and I found my friends, the mourners, already seated in the Church. Frank was there and so was Will Prothero. There were coaches for the mourners but F. brough this car and kindly offered the vicar and me a seat. The vicar with a gracious gesture transmitted to my understanding a repetition of the demonstration of the "dust" [before the broom] story and so in his polite way surrendered the seat on the right. All seated we set out on our 19 mile journey. My companion was very affable, and I enjoyed the conversation about various subjects as we followed the course of the river Taff with its delightful views "ever changing ever new." When next you visit our country I must take you up there.

Having reached the place where we were to alight, a former vicar of M.V. was there and took part in the service at the grave side. As we stood there someone touched my arm and on looking in that direction, Campbell, Peggy's brother was the foremost figure. The inscription on the piece of metal that was fixed to the front of the casket certified that the departed had reached the age of 80 years. I thought, and still think, how true are placed the words—"Swift to its close ebbs out life's little day."

The place names alone made we want to steal the bike of the soldiers again and take off. In the rest of the letter I returned straight to Greenmeadow:

> Don't drink, don't smoke is my maxim. I have always been able to do without either of these luxuries. Keep a good thick sole under your feet and allow your boots no leakage. If nails are wanted then decorate the soles! Shaped pegs are alright for when worn can be replaced.

And after this advice, Uncle expressed his concern for me and, as always, held out a helping hand:

We are thirsting to know how far you are from the "bus," the time you leave home in the morning, and the time of return. If you think my brown suit will fit you, let me know and I will send it along ,and anything else that is mine. Please tell your good mother we hope she will yield part of her claim to you in order that we may be joint owners. Dinky and Dilly are as usual. Dilly supervising whatever work is in progress.

I quoted so much of this letter because it is perhaps Uncle William's best self portrait.

I did not ask Uncle William to send me his suit, nor anything else, but he sent clothes anyway. And when "the Quakers collected clothes," not for Aberdare, but for the students in Vienna, I got my very first suit. The striped tie that Uncle had sent me—it looked very much like the one he wears in the picture—went very well with the dove grey material of the suit.

Registered you a letter on the 5th inst.   Greenmeadow
Posted parcel on the 7th Llanfedwy Cardiff
     Wales

Our Dear John,
     To say we were glad to have news of you again hardly reaches the positive degree.
     Dear generous heart. As it was your more kind intention of making me the custodian of the beautiful little plaque, you have made it difficult for me to find appropriate words to convey to you my feeling of thankfulness. All my best thanks please accept.
     Your dear letter of some time ago led me to understand that you come short of wearing apparel! Well, in response we posted to your address some worn clothing. And, in order that you may be able to check the number and kind of garment, I now give you a list of those articles that were enclosed: trousers, shirt, 2 pairs of woollen stockings. For your dear mother Auntie enclosed 1 pair stockings, a pair of woollen gloves, a black jumper and slip to wear under. Possibly you will recognize some of them!

Forgive more now won't you. A longer letter soon. All our love to your dear Mother and self.

Your affectionate Uncle and Auntie

Christmas Eve 1946

Guess who we are longing to be here with us now!!! It appears that we are allowed to send you worn (!) clothing. As there is more wear on the inside than on the outside of the leg of a trousers the piece of material has been put on to take the rub. Included in the parcel were three books Ernie brought here and the one you left here.

One of the books was *On the Art of Writing* by Sir Arthur Quiller-Couch which Uncle William had shown to me at Greenmeadow, and I also "recognized some of the clothes": As I unpacked the pepper-and-salt pants that I had worn on that walk up Craig Llysfaen I was right there on our "hill" with Viv. Not that I needed any special reminder of her. She wrote many long letters to Austria; she sent food parcels, and she sent books. She wanted to know what course I was taking. Soon I received a book related to it, whether it was Jespersen's *Language* or *Hamlet*, an *Old English Reader* or Bertrand Russell. I had to get good grades to keep my exemption from tuition status. Viv's interest in my studies and unstinting support were a constant encouragement.

Greenmeadow
7 February 1947

Dear One-of-us.

It was a relief yesterday morning to be assured of your most kind letter–long looked for–that you are now the owners of the few articles we intended should become your property. Today we feel quite light hearted, and satisfied, that you and your dear Mother are well–after a period of longing! Viv sent on your reply cablegram knowing it would ease our minds. She has not been out here for about three weeks. Ernie was pleased to tell us, when he was here, some little time ago, that he had received a letter from you, in fact, he brought it with him for us to read. It is intensely cold. I have a job to guide the quill. We are very pleased to be informed that you are getting on with your studies. Our thoughts are with you every day. With these beautiful souvenirs constantly reminding us. When your temporary abode was near here you could come over as often as you were inclined to give us that pleasure.

All our love to your dear Mother and self,

your Aff. Auntie & Uncle.

The months passed, the years. Uncle William's letters kept my memory alive of that by now magical spring of 1946. And he always recalled our time together and our parting which never failed to evoke his nostalgia. One day he made me see Greenmeadow as I had never seen it:

17 March St. P. 1947

Our beloved John and Mother,

Since the receipt on the 4h inst. of your longed for, and very kind letter, for which I now thank you, we have been enveloped in the atmosphere of some far-distant region— Snow to right of us, snow to the left of us, snow overhead and under! Neither of us seems to remember such piled up quantities! The second fall came before the first had quite gone. The panorama on Sat. morning last left a lasting impression—the glorious orb shone out in all its brilliance on the snow-covered country—a few clouds were driving over from the West, and the rest of the sky was a perfect blue. No matter what takes place under, the beautiful blue sky covers all! Our friends—some of the best in the world—Ernie among them look after us and do what they can to make things easier for us.

Being told by one of these neighbours that the drifted snow was filling up the road which you have often crossed, I went over on a Sunday morning to see for myself. In places the surface of the road after the snow had frozen and did not give way under my weight. When I reached the "farewell" gate—which was open—I looked in and saw that the snows had drifted to the top of the wall. To the left of the gate as I emerged from the enclosure, the roadway was full of this unusual deposit—even with the tops of the hedges! Traffic of any description was impossible. But I got on to the top of it and walked along a few paces, finding a level that will not last! I have mentioned this, John, because the spot is familiar to you.

One item in your letter brought us comfort and that was that your "feet are warm all day long." And we were thrilled by your description of the Danube!

The laburnum is now making an inward preparation for an outward display a little later on. Conspicuous among the trees is the "flame tree" which in the sun's glare, at this time of year, resembles a big flame going up. Our little squirrel has survived the severe frost. I saw it the other day leaping about the garden. The footpaths leading to this abode were obliterated by the depth of snow so with spade and shovel we set out to redefine the well-worn ways.!

This letter was started some days ago and I must not keep you waiting for a reply any longer. Please let me know if you would like a pair of stockings, with pretty tops–to wear with your knickers–one a fairly light pair and the other dark. The snow has almost gone, I am thankful to say.

With all our love to you both.

Your affectionate Auntie and Uncle.

The combustive power in coal does not bring it an inch nearer our gate! We still have to carry it from the deposit without the help of John and Paul.

31 May 1947

Dear One of us and your dear Mother,

[…]This time last year you were included in our family gathering but this year the laburnum lacks your admiration–only pink and yellow blooms this far, the purple has yet to make its appearance. How we wish you were here with us this afternoon. Your Auntie and I have been very busy preparing the land for the reception of the things we want to grow.[...]

A letter from Aunt Mary:

Dear John,

This is Green Meadow calling Vienna. How are you this morning? I hope you and all your kith and kin are well. We are very well. I thank you very much for all your nice kindly letters. We had such pleasure in reading them, and we shall hope to hear from you again soon. We shall look out every day for a letter from you from your home address. Soon I hope you will be looking at your beloved mountains. See "Everlasting Hills." Some people prefer the sea, but give me the hills and mountains. They remind me of the words "I will lift up mine eyes unto the hills from whence cometh my help." We have some very fine hills in Wales, and many glorious bits of landscape. We had a letter from Viv last week. She told us she would be returning to Newport on Monday last, and was looking for a visit to GM Saturday–tomorrow. She is longing to see us. She has had a very pleasant holiday. We have not seen Mr. and Mrs. B. for some time. Ernie has not called lately; he is very busy and works late, so we are told—we will envoy your message to him. Well, John, we shall always be very interested to hear of your doings, and as you journey through life remember the words "I shall pass through this world but once." You know the rest, a little kindness here and there or a smile and a handshake will sometimes help a lonely soul. "And the little we can do let us do it now." Dinky and Dilly are flourishing. Dilly is a mischievous little thing, but she's very knowing and intelligent (every evening about 7:00 she comes along, and if I'm sitting down she touches me with her little paw, as much as to say, give me my supper). Time is ½ to 9:00 a.m. and I must away to work. Thank you for the pleasure of your company, and hoping we shall meet you again one day. All the best to you wherever you may be.

With love from your aff. Auntie

One day in May 1949 I received again one of Viv's packages of books, and Alun Lewis' *Raiders' Dawn* was among them. Viv knew that I wanted to write my dissertation on a modern Welsh writer. She liked Lewis' poetry because critics had likened him to Keats and considered him one "who had risen beyond disillusionment." The poems that I "understood" most readily did not confirm such an assessment; they were those about Welsh mining villages, a Wales I had never seen. My courses in nineteenth-century English literature and my own working class background had directed my interest to social problems, and I had written a thesis on Disraeli's *Two Nations* and Kingsley's *Alton Lock*. I could feel my way into these poems because of my childhood during the Depression in Austria.

There was another reason why I was fascinated with Lewis. Listening to lectures about English and German literature at the University of Vienna I never heard anything about poets who had written about the war that had just ended, and like the British journalists in 1939/1940, I could ask in 1946/47: Where are the War Poets? Nobody talked about the war in literature. And here was this Welshman who had. Lewis had been born ten years before me, but was one of the war generation, and he was a soldier "on the other side," the side I had become interested in at Ruperra. How had he experienced the war? How had he written about it? I did not look at his work as an academic challenge; I wanted to see parallels with my own experience. I was looking for a modern writer I could relate to. But I realized how different Lewis's war had been from mine. He experienced it as a poet, and my all too literal reading, trying to discover correspondences, could not grasp what he was trying to say. I needed time, needed more exposure to modern poetry, before I could approach him critically as a dissertation would require me to do.

Back To Wales

1949 was a decisive year. I had read Alun Lewis for the first time, I finished most of my courses for the teacher's diploma, and I came back to Wales, this time not through the kind cooperation of the British Army but the generosity of the British Council. After a summer program at St. Andrews, I was looking forward to being in Wales again. What would it be like to walk around Ruperra Castle grounds as a free man, a nostalgic tourist so to speak? Viv had been there not too long before:

> I strolled up to Ruperra Castle the other evening and found it exactly as you described it in your letter. I stood there gazing for a while at the view down to the Channel All is deserted now but everywhere is evidence of your sojourn there. The sentry box still stands at the upper entrance and the forbidding notice remains: No Admittance. Keep Out!

The huts are there. Nothing has been done. All is just as you left it almost twelve months ago. It was a beautiful evening, clear and lovely. Yes, the bluebells, primroses and milkmaids make a pretty garden along the banks of the top road, and the array of trees is magnificent.

I was especially looking forward to seeing my old friends at Greenmeadow again. I knew I would be welcome.

Greenmeadow
Llanfedwy
Cardiff, S. Wales
9th July 1949

Our beloved John and Mother,

Well, old man, how are you? Viv tells us that you have been working hard with your studies–the reward for such hard work will soon be made known. Those happy hours of three years ago are still vivid–

> Swiftly our pleasures glide away.
> Our hearts recall the distant day
> With many sighs!
> The moments that are speeding past
> We heed not but the past –the past–
> More highly prize.

We are experiencing very dry, warm weather and this morning, the well here being dry–I had to carry water from the "Amazon." It is possible that we shall meet again ere long. So get together all the good news about your dear self which we shall be anxious to hear. Is it possible to gain your forgiveness for keeping you all this time without use of the quill?

All our love from Aunt Mary and
Your affectionate Uncle William

Viv is here and has kindly promised to post this letter.

I saw Greenmeadow again and called the dear old people uncle and auntie. Uncle William took me along to a Council meeting, but to his dismay

I was not allowed to listen to the proceedings. Then we went to the National Museum in Cardiff where I saw that painting of a Welsh miner. A few weeks later, his letter, in his handwriting, his literary style with the quotations, a style that was not affected because it was his nature, the details, his warmth and the edgy strokes of the quill recaptured for me once more the spirit of Greenmeadow of 1946.

Greenmeadow
Llandedwy
Michaelston-y-Fedwy
9th January 1950

Our beloved John and Mother.

If it is admissible for me to quote at my heart's dictation from a letter recently received from my life-long friend, the Prebendary of St. Paul's, the opening sentence is – "It did me a world of good to see your clear and distinct script again," and indeed it did me good to see your good handwriting once again! And the manner in which you have constructed some of the sentences makes me feel quite proud of you, John! After the long absence it was lovely to set eyes on you again, and to hear once again the familiar voice!

Sorry we were that the time spent with us was so short- better luck next time, let's hope. The two 'terrified ladies' [guests whom I had accompanied to the bus] make kind enquiries after you when I see them, and they think how fortunate they were to have your manly company during that raging storm! With them you are a favourite. Miss Wolfe claims some connection with Gen. Wolfe of Quebec fame.

Your pretty card, for which please accept my thanks, has been admired by the friends who called here. How glad we were to be assured of your success, and we trust "that your efficient services may be prolonged at the fount of knowledge." Apparently the photo was a failure. The next time you come we must try to get a camera and arrange a group including Dilly and Dinky on the front. I hope we shall go to the Museum together again and spend a little longer time in its walls. My mischeevius friend passed away into oblivion on the 12th of No. last, and was cremated. He loved being here with us.

> Time steals them from us–chances strange
> That come to all
> Some in the most exalted state
> Relentless sweeps the stroke of fate
> The strongest fall.

Some time ago there was a general appeal from the Master of the Rolls asking people to preserve old letters and documents. A meeting in connection with the appeal was held in the Assembly Rooms, in the County Hall, Cardiff, which I, among many others, had been invited to attend. The invitation cards were embellished with the names of two popular gentlemen who were to address the gathering. Owing to my rather defective hearing, and the reechoing of voices, I was unable to bring away with me even one complete sentence of the proceedings! I hope other listeners were more fortunate.

Well, old man, a letter from you will always be welcome at this address, so collect all the news you can.

All my love and best wishes through the approaching year to your good mother and self

Your affectionate Uncle William

I saw Viv in Newport. But there was no time to see the Castle again. As in 1945, 1946; the people were more important than that old shell of former glory. Ernie enjoyed so much taking me on his motorcycle for a beer in a pub way up on a hill.

I had written to Gweno Lewis, and she had invited me to see her one day after her school day at Mountain Ash. We talked in the house where Alun had come home on leave and I even met Bombo the black Tomcat. I told Mrs. Lewis what I was hoping to do, and she immediately helped and promised more help. And that was the beginning of our correspondence that has lasted to this day. Indeed, 1949 was an important year for me.

It also brought back Fiona. After our last clandestine meeting near Ruperra Castle we had not been in contact. Once back in Austria I wrote her, and we carried on a rather irregular correspondence. Now that I was going to be in Wales I wanted to see her again. I took a bus to Trethomas and saw her briefly. The old temptation returned, but her mother came home, and I had to get my bus back to Newport. I never saw her again. But our correspondence revived for a while. Fiona represented a side of Wales that could not have been more different from the tranquility and timelessness of Greenmeadow. She was only three years younger than I, and her letters were typical of students' letters in their mixture of banter, flirtation, moments of profundity, and real concerns about her studies; she wasn't very happy at school but seems to have finally settled down at Cardiff Technological College. She had taken English, had wanted to write, then changed to economics, got interested in the Fabian Society and Marxist utopian ideas. She sent me the text of the latest hits that I had asked her for–I still had that song in my ears that she had sung in the spring of 1946; in her long letters she included quotations from Tennyson, and Omar Khayyam whom she admired; a beautiful passage by Joseph Conrad about his first encounter with spoken English, an homage to love by H.G. Wells, the melancholy "The night has a thousand eyes"–"by some French bloke," –and once when she was very depressed, she quoted Alun Lewis. She had met somebody who had known Lewis, but nothing came of that contact, nor of her plans to come to Austria. She didn't have the money. She thought that I should come to England and teach German (years before I ended up doing that in the States!). Fiona was witty, critical, and refreshingly direct. About the food situation in 1947 she wrote to me in Austria: "You cannot be much worse off than we are, but we don't deserve it." Her letters were often amusing; she told me not to miss the latest hit "My Foolish Heart," but was honest when she said that she found it difficult to "write slush, and lies." I regret that, probably due to my negligence and my new start in the States, our correspondence broke off. When now after fifty years, being the "sentimentalist" that she called me, I tried to find her, she had disappeared.. Her last letter was written in May 1951, five years after our secret meeting:

> I went to the castle about a week ago, but unfortunately there were no flowers there. The weather has been so bad. I think the frost had killed most of them. I was very disappointed. Though, it was worth it, if just to bring back old memories, and the place is still as beautiful as ever.

That September of 1949 I had gone to Trethomas a second time to see her but we missed each other. She was late, and I had an appointment with J. B. Morse, the Rilke scholar who had translated Alun Lewis's "To Rilke" for one of the very first postwar literary magazines in Austria. I had my first talk with a scholar who knew Alun Lewis's work and, though I don't recall what we talked about, I remember how jovial Morse was. "In memory of a happy evening in the Continental in Cardiff" he later sent me his article on "Rainer Maria Rilke and English Literature," my first piece of secondary literature for my dissertation.

On my way back to Vienna I dropped in at Allen and Unwin's in London and told them of my dissertation plans with the hope that they might give me the other books by Lewis which they had published. I bought them, and started reading them as the train went through France and through the Alps to Vienna. Of the stories in *The Last Inspection* the stories in Part Two about poor Welsh people touched me as the poems had done—their common denominator: poverty—and resignation, rebellion, frustration.

And the stories about the soldiers in England! How I wished I had read them at Ruperra, when I could have talked to our guards about them. They were not stories about action in battle but about army life more like that at Ruperra, the army routine. Now I could see our Sergeant Major, Taffy, even that mysterious lieutenant as characters in Lewis's stories. But biographical links even beyond "enemy lines" are not sufficient to do justice to the stories. There was so much more, and there was India, completely unknown to me. I could only attempt to understand it as Lewis had transformed it in his art. I needed more time, more exposure to modem literature and criticism; under the system at the University of Vienna I had no guidance. The only encouragement from my dissertation Professor was that he accepted my topic in spite or because of the fact that Lewis was unknown in Austrian research of English Literature. My academic needs blended with my desire to get away from Austria for a while (my relationship with Ilse had had too many ups and downs), and I was delighted to be awarded a Fulbright scholarship to the US. I studied British and American literature at the University of Minnesota.

Again I was in a different world, with new people and a partly new language. No one in Minneapolis wrote or spoke Uncle William's English. I bought myself a Smith Corona typewriter, because hardly anybody wrote by hand, let alone with a quill. But the old magic reached me even there:

Greenmeadow, Christmas 1951

Our beloved John,
> Onward its course the present keeps.
> Onward the constant current sweeps,
>> Till life is done!
> Could we but judge of time aright
> The past and future in their flight
>> Would be as one.

Your spirit, John, appears to be disturbing something responsive within me and I must delay writing no longer. If this reply is delayed I cannot forget the happy hours you shared with us. To see you again would be to us a great pleasure as you know.

This morning we became possessed of your dear letter which, with those of previous receptions, will be preserved and read again and again!! We are delighted to hear that you are well and making progress in the New World. You will have much to tell us when next you come along. ….

You are aware of my visit to the hospital where an operation took place immediately after arrival and where I was detained until 19. June 1950 having entered the 15 March previously.

Good Ernie was very attentive through the period of indisposition. He is the "Good Samaritan," anything he could do, day or night. Now here is a story no one else can relate to you. When the days were long, fairly early one morning Auntie happened to be leaning on the gate at the back between our paddock and the adjoining field. A little brown squirrel came along climbing up over her and leaped into the hedge. Could such an incident ever happen again?!

Mr. Blackbum, you will be sorry to hear died a few months ago.

When I got up from my seat in the Council chamber the other afternoon, The Chairman who is a friend of ours, halted the proceedings to express his own and the wishes of the other members "A Happy Christmas" to your Uncle and Aunt. Such a lovely greeting was very unexpected for we had already received a card with good wishes from the Chairman and his wife.

If I go on writing I may lose the post so must give the quill a rest. Well, old man, may you be a partaker in the best that the season provides. All our love,

Your affectionate Uncle and Auntie

Uncle William's next and last letter greeted me in Austria on my "return from the Land of Study and Travel" in August of 1952. Greenmeadow was unchanged. Neighbours had come by, Ernie and Viv had come to see them. There had been some sickness, some funerals. "Dame Nature" had had her moods:. "Some weeks ago our well in the garden became waterless and then we had to climb down the slope and interrupt the flow of the Amazon!! The downpour of late had brought back the spring.

"Dilly" and "Donk" are as usual, making victims of the mice that come within their reach." The most sensational news Uncle had quilled at the very top of the first page to ensure my immediate attention. "The composition of the competitions for the crown at the National Eidsteddfod was not up to standard and so the 'head' decoration was not awarded!!"

Of greater importance to me than the Eisteddford was that I, as Uncle put it, "had contacted some friendly folk in life's way." One of the friendly folk, a student of English, followed me to Vienna six months later. I started teaching full time to keep Lois and myself, if not in clover, so at least in oats and occasional raisins. After school I worked on the dissertation on Alun Lewis. Wales was close to me in this work, not only a treasured memory ever refreshed by the letters. Greenmeadow had become my private myth. My discovery of it in that summer of 1946 was in some quiet way what the orange grove was to the soldier in Lewis's story, an "enlargement of the imagination." At least I like to think of it that way.

Viv wrote on 13th April 1954:

> I go out to Greenmeadow fairly frequently on Saturdays. Uncle you would find very changed in appearance. He is frail and cannot maintain his one-time inexhaustible supply of amusing and informative anecdotes. He quickly tires but never complains. He says he mustn't complain. Uncle I know regrets that now he may never see you again. Time passes quietly, peacefully for them delighting as they do in

the simple everyday things of life. A Mrs. Evans comes and tidies the place for them. It is as much as they can do to do the little necessary jobs. The poultry are diminished to five hens and the sheep have been sold for Aunty could no longer cope. But I learn much. Their life is full of a quiet strength and courage which springs from their deep faith in the ultimate good.

My letters must have upset her; she knew how my life had changed but was concerned that I would stray from the high course she had set for me:

Why this awful fever for work? What is driving you? Have you forgotten how beautiful it is to be still and at peace at times. But what a raging turmoil you seem to be in. I suggested a study of Alun Lewis for he was a man after my own heart, one who to my thinking and feeling had put the right things first. You know the phrase —"Seek ye first the Kingdom of God." To me Alun Lewis did just that. I wanted you to become like him.

My dissertation was accepted in the summer of 1954. I would certainly write it differently now. My teachers in Minneapolis preached the New Criticism and I did learn to "read closely." But by not considering other approaches, so much was left unsaid.

. . . And Back Again

We celebrated my degree in 1955 with a bicycle trip to England and on to Wales. We passed through Steep, saw the house in which Edward Thomas had lived and climbed the hill where Alun Lewis had sat and written:

> I sat and watched the dusky berried ridge
> Of yew trees, deepened by oblique dark shafts,
> Throw back the flame of red and gold and russet
> That leapt from beech and ash to birch and chestnut
> Along the downward arc of the hill's shoulder....

We crossed the bridge into Wales at Chepstow, cycled past the Race Course where Camp 409 had been and along the Wye on a road that must have been the same on which we POWs had marched ten years before. In that miraculous summer—it rained one day in five weeks—we saw so much of beautiful Wales from Anglesey to the Gower Coast that ever since we have wanted to repeat the unrepeatable. In Aberystwyth we spent some lovely days with Gweno Lewis, her brother Hywel Ellis and their parents, and Hywel showed us the countryside he loves so much, We went to Ruperra, walked down the hill to Greenmeadow. Only Aunt Mary lived there now; Uncle had died the year before. It was a sad afternoon, but it was good to be there with Lois in the old house where it had all started: my English studies that eventually had taken me to Minneapolis where we had met. We went to the Michaelston churchyard to visit Uncle William's grave; there were several fresh graves, and the sexton had no idea which was which. I saw Viv in Newport; our friendship was saddened not only by Uncle William's death, but continued for a number of years. In 1962 she wrote: "In an outward sense Greenmeadow as we knew it exists no more yet, in our hearts and minds it lives vividly unchanged and unchangeable. I hope one day you will write a story about it." Viv had always overrated my abilities. I could only chronicle the fragile circumstances between war and peace, the confusion, hopes and uncertainty that would all have to be integrated in such a story.

With our move to the United States my professional life shifted again. Due to the new demand in foreign languages in the States, I taught German literature and language at the college level. And again I lived in two worlds. My everyday life was in the States; in my work I was back in Germany and Austria, especially the Austria before it had ceased to exist for twelve years. I was trying to understand how it had all happened, the economic, political, ideological pandemonium of that "low, dishonest decade," and how my generation had been pulled into its vortex. And I read Alun Lewis again. In 1938 when Hitler marched into Austria, he had written the poem "Anschluss." It opened with the words:

> They have clipped the wings of my doves, my messengers of delight,
> And they in whom I have delighted have been shackled with chains.
> They were sent to toil in the claypits, they have become quarriers of stones:
> The harp and the lute have been taken from their hands,
> They have forgotten their delight.

The pictures of Bergen Belsen that I had seen in Chepstow, Uncle Williams' question about German brutality demanded at last a response. I studied the work of Jura Soyfer, a young Austrian Jewish writer who, as a Marxist, had followed the "old temptation to remould the world" (Alun Lewis), had fought for the vision and paid for it with his life. On March 12, 1938 he had been "sent to toil" in the gravel pits of Dachau, and died in Buchenwald. He was twenty-six, three years younger than Alun Lewis. I read and thought about those who had been murdered as "quarriers of stone" in Mauthausen. All I could do was help keep their memory alive in my work and my students. I tried to combine my studies in German with my sustained reading of Alun Lewis, and wanted to make him known in German-speaking countries. I was not very successful and thought that a recommendation by Vernon Watkins might help.

The Garth
Pennard Cliffs
Near Swansea
South Wales
27th December, 1961

Dear Mr. Jarka,

Thank you for your letter. I am sorry to hear that the good German reviews will not take your translations of Alun Lewis, and I think it is their loss. I don't myself believe that Alun Lewis's voice is too quiet for the market in translations, as you suggest, but that those who run the stalls are probably too unenterprising. Your sustained feeling for his work over a long time is the best qualification for writing about him, and I hope your efforts to make him known in Germany will be successful. Mrs. Gweno Lewis, who has stayed here and whom you know, will be able to help you, especially as she understands German.

My own view is that a writer's work should first be translated, and then commented on. I do not think any critical angle should be set up in advance of the work itself. You will find Dylan Thomas's broadcast talk on Welsh poets in QUITE EARLY ONE MORNING, which Erich Fried has translated under the title IM JUNGEN MORGEN, I think (I lent the book a few weeks ago, so I forget the exact German title and it is significant that in these two pages he devotes to Alun Lewis, more than half of what he says is quotation.

My three sonnets A WREATH FOR ALUN LEWIS in my last book CYPRESS AND ACACIA were suggested when I received from Gweno Lewis an advance copy of the posthumous collection, IN THE GREEN TREE. You refer to one sonnet, probably the prefatory one which I wrote when I heard of his death, but I would like you also to know these three. I read the three-part poem at the Aberdare ceremony, a most moving and memorable day. I shall try to jot down a few lines with this letter, but I doubt whether they will help you in getting your translations accepted. I am also entirely Welsh, but my sonnets were prompted by an awareness of something more than a national loss.

Yours sincerely, Vernon Watkins

ALUN LEWIS

It is unusual to find in a poet killed before his thirtieth year a twofold promise such as the Welsh poet Alun Lewis possessed. Like Edward Thomas and Wilfred Owen in the war which preceded his own, he carried an invisible equipment in which a bitter awareness of the human condition and an intense compassion for people were welded togther. He was a witness and an interpreter. He refused to be adopted by any clique. Arriving in India in the humility of friendship and service and the solitude of his own imagination, he expressed, as no one else has done, the experience of these conditions which the common soldier could not communicate. The acute observation and penetration of his late prose and the sharp pathos of his verse were the outer facets of his own self-examination, a restless element which accompanied him everywhere. He knew already that if a poet listened to himself a nation would one day hear him; and he knew, too, that a prose writer could not lose himself too much in the activity of others.

Vernon Watkins

Years later *Neue Deutsche Hefte*, a respectable literary monthly published Lewis's "The Orange Grove" in my translation. I translated some of the poems, stories, and letters, and sent them to Biederstein Verlag, a Munich publisher who had brought out important German language authors. Biederstein 'was impressed by the work of "this author who had died all too soon," did an excellent thoughtful editing job, and, though not expecting big sales, gave me a contract for publication in 1971. Then the delays started. Poor sales of similar works by other authors made the publisher hesitate again and again, and when repeated attempts to place some of the shorter pieces in newspapers and radio to draw attention to this unjustly forgotten author failed, they took Lewis off their program for good. Changes in ownership had been another, perhaps decisive factor. The company was swallowed up by a corporation and could continue their own imprint only with a greatly reduced list of authors. After my long and detailed correspondence with Biederstein I am convinced of their sincerity when they expressed their disappointment and regret at not being able to publish Lewis in whose work I, as they put it, "had invested such intensity and competence."

Many years later, Selwyn Evans wrote in a letter to me: "Alun and I served in the South Wales Borderers and were friends. I was in the near vicinity when he died and was present at his burial and his funeral." Evans was in contact with the well-known Austrian poet Erich Fried who admired Alun's work, and through his many contacts was hoping to make Lewis known in Germany. At Fried's request I sent him my translations, but Fried's illness and death in 1987 stopped all these efforts. Considering the present publishing market in Germany, the hope that interest in Alun Lewis will be aroused is very dim indeed. Publishing giants like Bertelsmann are strong enough to buy up Random House and others but hardly interested in a book that would not sell 100,000 copies. Still, I have not given up all hope.

...And Again

It took me thirty years to come back to Wales–this time from the United States where we had moved in 1962. Of my friends at Greenmeadow only one was still alive, and my connection with that "paradise," as Uncle William called it, ended as it had begun–with Ernie. Over the years our correspondence had been reduced to the exchange of Christmas greetings, but with the prospects of a reunion he wrote more frequently.

> If you ever come to this country the door is open. Do you remember these words: "I shall pass through this world but once...." (February 1982)

Had a dream before Christmas. In my dream I had been to Blackburns, he was full of cancer and I used to go to the Doctor for whatever he wanted, so when I walked out from there I said to myself, I must go to Greenmeadow. Now in my dream it was a real summer day. Walking up through the Oaks it came to me it is no use going, Mr. and Miss Rees are both dead. The sun went out.

[...] My brother's daughter was up at the Castle last Sunday to pick snowdrops and she was telling her little girl about you boys who were there after the war. (February 15 1982)

I was very happy to have your letter for it brought back to me the happiest years of my life going to Blackburns and then to Greenmeadow. (April 12 1982)

Greenmeadow is still much the same as it was when you were there except that some of the big oaks in the paddock are gone. Miss Rees had them cut down and sold them to a smart boy who never paid for them. It was a blow for her; those trees were worth a lot of money. It upset her very much. Myself, I did not like the thought of them being cut down for they were very old, but they were not mine or they would still be there. Only God can make a tree. (April 22, 1982)

I was up at the Castle last week and there was no one about at all only the trees and they make no noise, so it is grand to go round there for a walk. (23 June 82)

When I look at the trees with autumn tints the thought of the cold weather makes me sad for I can't get about when the roads are bad. The wanderlust gets me, can never stay in, must be out. Some day I do hope we will meet again and wander through those grand old woods. (August 14 1982)

Some day may be we shall walk around the Castle that would be grand. Am going to watch the Rugby International between Wales and England; the wild men from the mountains of Wales will be there in full song. Cardiff will be busy tonight. (February 5 1983)

I do hope you will be able to come to the old country some time for I will be glad to see you all. Am going to Aberystwyth next week up with the wild men, coming back down on the 18th for the big rugby match. The singing before the match is very often better than the game. You should hear the Welsh crowd sing. (February 1 1984)

This is the chap you met at Blackburns so long ago. I will never forget those days or the words "I shall pass through this world but once. Any kindness that I can show any human being let me not delay it or defer it for I shall not pass this way again" —I was young then, an old man now. (December 1984)

Our walk will be about seven miles so do hope the sun will shine every day you are here. Will be very glad to walk with you for I know you will enjoy going around again once more the walks you know. On our way back from our walk we will call at the Cefn Mably Arms and I will buy you a pint of Welsh beer for by the time we get there we will both be *thirsty* and it will go down fine (June 6 1985)

We stayed with Ernie at Rhyd-y-Gwern. His niece took us around in her car. Again we went to Ruperra Castle which was by now in much worse condition than it was in my memory. I even found the path again up my "poetry hill," though the trees were too high to allow any views. Some of the rhododendrons were still blooming among the tumbled-down stones of the wall at the top. The tree with the inscription "I shall not pass this way again..." I did not find. But Ernie confessed shyly that he had carved it in 1945 or 46. I should have known. He lived what he had carved. As promised, he took us for a pint of ale at the Cefn Mably Arms. The Greenmeadow I knew was no more. A huge electric transmission tower had been put up next to the cottage and dwarfed it. The garden was a wilderness, the house in bad repair; we did not go in. Some halfhearted restoration work seemed to be in progress. Rusty gutter supports were lying around in the rubble. I picked one up to take with me. "What do you want that for?" asked Ernie's niece. What for indeed?

***

This was the melancholy ending that my story inevitably led up to. The dear people who were so kind to me at Greenmeadow had been dead for years: Uncle William and Aunt Mary, Viv, and Ernie. They could not read what I had written in their memory. And the people who might read it now never knew them in person. I put the manuscript aside, a closed book. A few months later it was opened again. I had underestimated the power of memory. I received a letter from Roger Jones, Viv's nephew, little Roger who had sat on my knees that summer day in 1946, jubilantly opening my fist again and again:

> "…I have recently retired from my work as civil engineer at sixty, and in tidying my papers came across your letter of February 28, 1985. Many happy memories flooded back of our meetings at Greenmeadow in 1946 where you were with William and Mary helping them at their cottage…"

I don't remember the letter Roger refers to; I must have written it the year when Lois and I were about to come to Wales, and I had hoped to see him again. For some reason or other nothing came of that or any other reunion. Every time I had returned to Wales we had missed each other. Roger had been very close to Viv, and from her letters I knew how delighted she was with her bright, vivacious little nephew. She often reported his triumphs in school and their adventures together.

> Roger spends a good bit of his spare time with me; often he comes out to Greenmeadow on Saturdays. Uncle is delighted with his company. Roger has a taste for things old, churches, cathedrals etc. etc. He's fascinated when Uncle entertains him with one of his discourses on ancient ways and customs. He's going to dig round about Greenmeadow to see if he can unearth some piece of pottery, china or some coins, even a stone ax head maybe.

Greenmeadow was the bond between the three of us, and when Viv and Roger were not out there, he was the only one she could talk to about me reinforcing the memory of that one afternoon (or had it been really more than one?). One day a child's letter was enclosed in Viv's, and we, the little Welsh boy and the former POW and now university student and middle school teacher, became pen pals. "He made quite an impression when he announced in school that you were Austrian," Viv commented. The recent surprise letter from sixty-year-old Roger made me search for the letters he had written as a boy. I think I found most of them. They reflect the passing years as the careful printing of the early ones became a hurried slanted longhand until the teenager outgrew handwriting and childhood, and advanced to using his brother's typewriter.

In a letter of 1953, Roger wrote: "Uncle William has been quite ill during the past few weeks, but yesterday Aunty said that he was looking much better and wanting to get up. Three lambs have been born in Uncle's orchard and are now quite big. Thank you very much for the stamps you sent me, I didn't have about six of them and I am going to swap the rest of them soon. Lately Aunty Viv and I have been going on expeditions to various places…"

Uncle William died in 1954, and Roger did not mention Greenmeadow any more. Schoolwork filled his letters. And, as I informed Viv of my progress at the university, Roger wrote me about his examinations. He was an excellent student and still a boy of course:

> Sometimes I play with the catapult you gave me when I was younger. The original elastic has, unfortunately, broken, but I have mended it with new aeroplane elastic. I also have the Austrian hunting knife, and I am now allowed to use it…. Also I have been youth hosteling as you have, and I planned to go to Storey Arms where you stayed. …Our pet Corgy, is very nice, and he is now barking at the cat next door. He is a lovely red color, with a white chest and four white paws. Nearly every day I take him for a walk to the fields which lie above our house, and there he can run around off the lead.
>
> I am sending you, as requested, a picture of our little corgi. His name by the way, is Shon, pronounced Shorn. This is the Welsh equivalent for John. I am sorry you could not read it in my last letter. My handwriting isn't very good, indeed, in school, none of my friends can read it. I do not do much German in school, so it would not be worth your while to try to help me, and my vocabulary is limited to such words as Spritsflasche, filtrierpapier, and becherglas…
>
> P.S. Shon is only a foot high, if you should wonder.

That was Roger's last letter. He was sixteen. As his childhood receded more and more our correspondence broke off. I have put Roger's letters all together as the special group they were. Uncle William's letters came from a different age, Viv's came from a busy schoolteacher's everyday world though they rose above it in their exuberant idealism and warm affection. Roger's letters brought me the freshness of childhood, its fun and humour, a timeless innocence that in a strange way connected them to the simplicity that I had found in Greenmeadow. It is this connection that makes them more than an epilogue to my story.

Half a century after our meeting in that idyllic place, Roger writes: "Aunty Viv and I used to catch the bus from Newport to Cefn Mably, then walk what seemed a long, long way to Greenmeadow, up a long straight road, then off on a footpath crossing a stream and up to the farm to be greeted by the geese…"

I am there with him. It's good to know that Greenmeadow still exists in at least one more living memory.

Next Few Pages: Sketches and Letters by Roger Jones as He Was Growing Up, Sent to Horst from Wales

10 Anthsury Rd
Newport
Mon

Dear John,
Thank-you for the letter you sent me. I was very pleased that you liked my drawing of the Royal Wedding.

I am quite well now thank-you. I have been going to school as usual, but now it is the Easter holiday. I am having a grand time learning to row. David and I have been to the canal for two days. Our favourite boat is called Red-Tulip. We find it the esiest to handle. The boat-man told us that people sometimes fall in as they step into the boat. The first time we went to the canal Daddy nearly fell in. He put his two legs into the boat which moved away quickly and Daddy was left with his fet in the boat and his hands on the bank. Daddy was saved from falling into the water by one man and three ladies pulling him back on to the bank. He looked ackuly funny. I ran to tell mummy.

Yester-day we had six little bunnies. One is pink and the other five are all black

When they grow older we shall be busy getting them food. They eat a carrier full each meal. A few days ago in the night Chinny the fierce Father Bunnie bit a large hole in his hutch, when we woke up in the morning he was in the garden playing so now he is in the old hutch, he will not be able to get out of that hutch, because the wood is strong and thick.

I have drawn you a picture of an Engine running through the coal fields of south Wales.

Please will you send me another letter very very soon.

I am tired now, this is the longest letter I have ever written.

With lots of love
and xxxx
from

Roger.

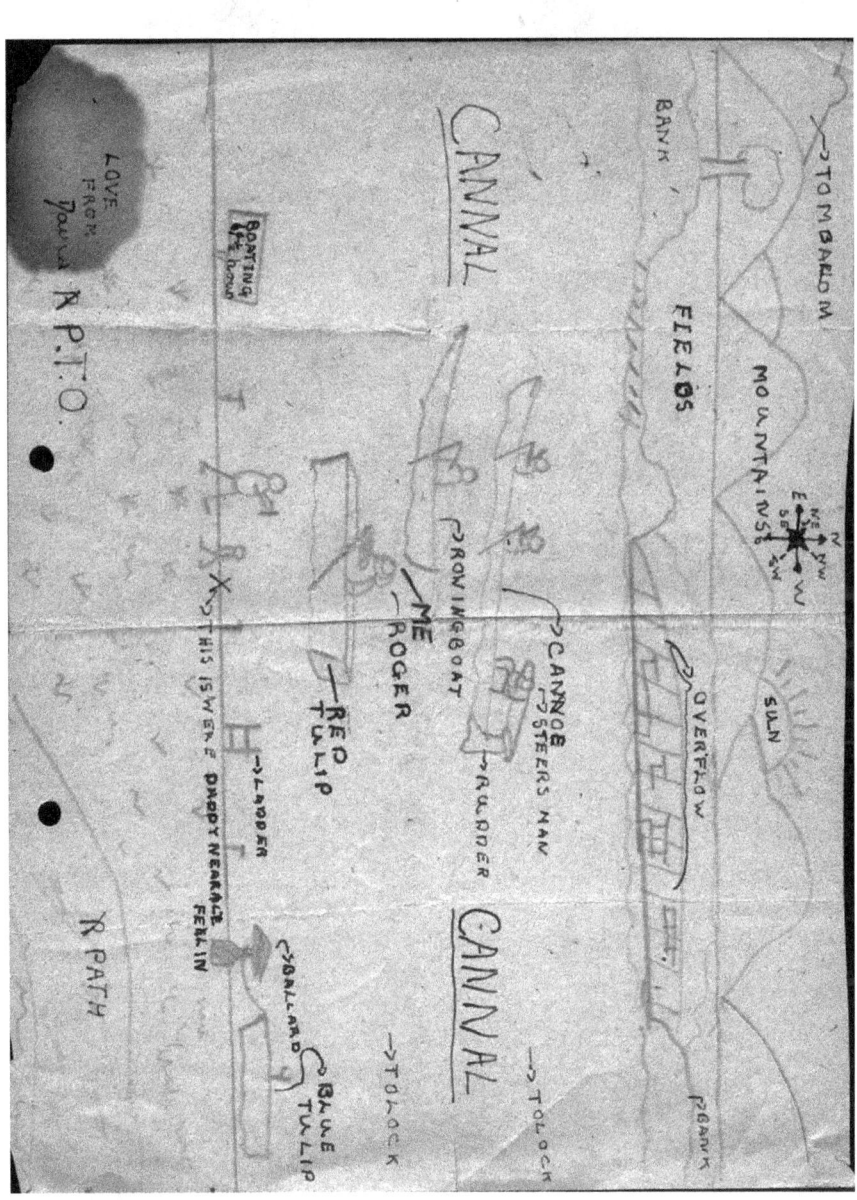

Roger as a Boy

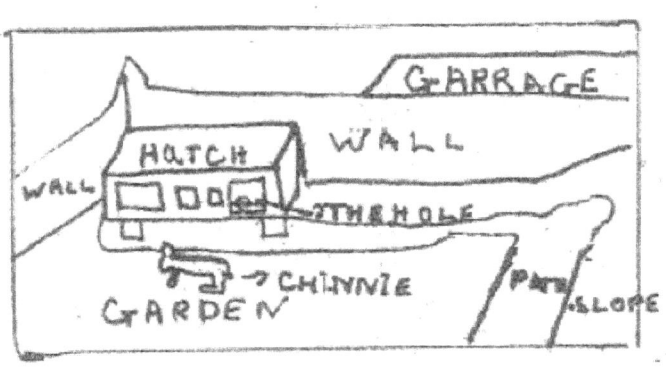

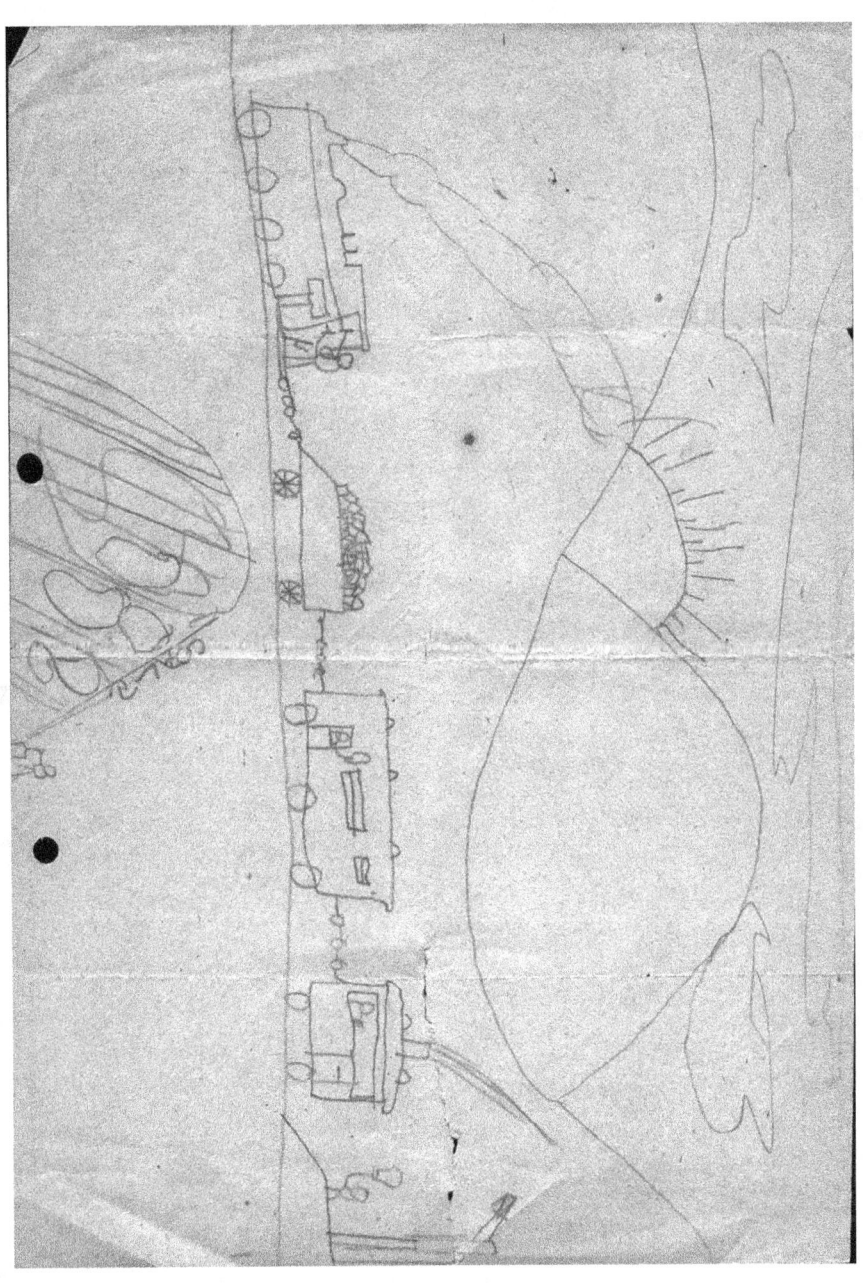

This and Following Pages: Letters to "John" (i.e., Horst) from Roger

10 Llanthewy Road
Newport
Mon
Dear John   November 14. 1943
    Thank-you very much for the knife you gave me for my birthday. I am going to wait until I am a boy scout then I will be able to hang it on my belt. About two weeks ago Chinny our rabbit escaped from his hutch and a police constable found him at 5.30 in the morning. We were very worried so at dinner time David went to the police station to see if the police knew anything about him. To his great delight Chinny was there, and the policeman told David how he had caught him. It was a stern chase with Chinny hopping frantically away, and the policeman diving wildly after him.
November 5th was Guy Fawkes night. As you know Guy Fawkes was the man who tried to blow up Parliament in the year 1605. Ever since we have celebrated the failure

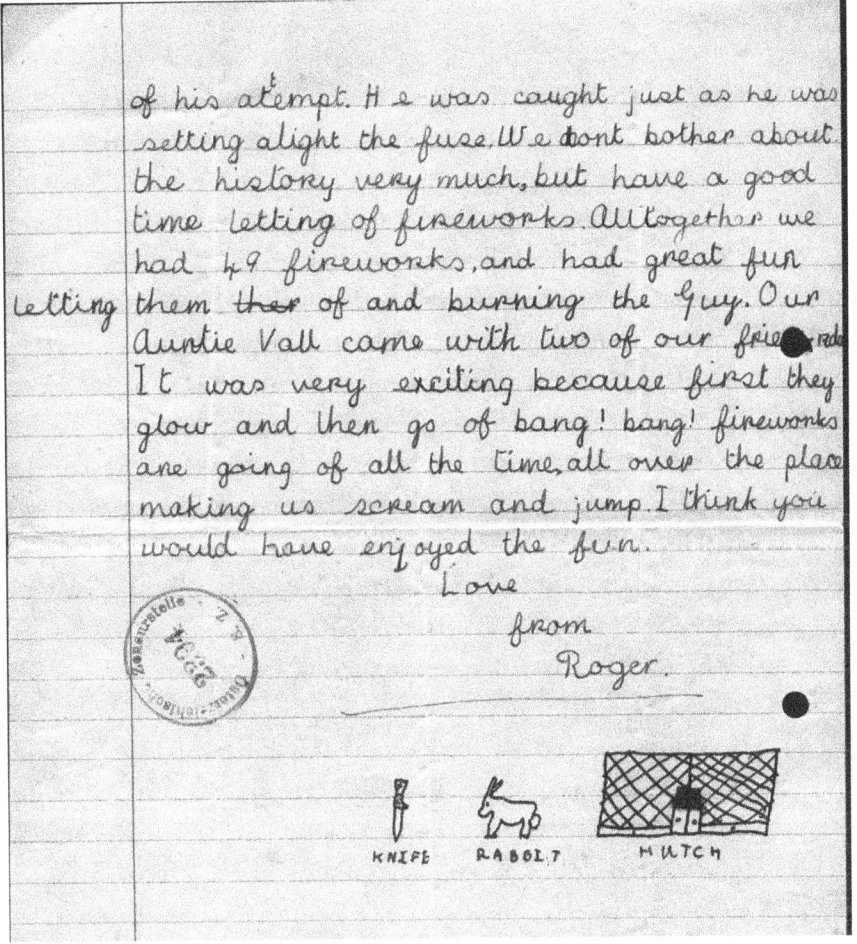

of his atempt. He was caught just as he was setting alight the fuse. We dont bother about the history very much, but have a good time letting of fireworks. Alltogether we had 49 fireworks, and had great fun letting them ther of and burning the Guy. Our Auntie Vall came with two of our frie~rds It was very exciting because first they glow and then go of bang! bang! fireworks are going of all the time, all over the place making us scream and jump. I think you would have enjoyed the fun.

        Love
          from
            Roger.

KNIFE   RABBIT   HUTCH

10 Llanthewy Rd
Newport
Mon.
20 November 46

Dear John,
Thank you very much for the catapult you left for me when you returned home. I was so glad to have your super catapult. Mummy says I am not to take it out but can shoot pellets of paper with it in the garden. So you see John, I can't use it much but I keep it with my other treasure, the jack-knife which you sent me from Vina.

I am so sorry I have not written to you sooner. I certainly should have. I was very disappointed when I came to Aunty's and found that you were gone. I wanted you to come and see us again. I stayed with Aunty Viv for the October holiday. We had a very good time together and Aunty took me out every day.

We went to Monmouth to see the Nelson Museum but it was closed until further notice, we were very disappointed but cheered up when we found we could go inside the old tower on the Monnow Bridge. Wasn't it lucky that Auntie saw the notice on the outside of a tiny shop saying Key for Monnow Bridge kept here. It was very interesting to see where the soldiers had poured down molten lead on the attacking enemy, and where they had pushed the condemned prisoners down the dungeon straight into the river.

We went to St Fagan's again and watched the wood-turner making spoons, bowls and plates. Aunty W Viv bought an ashtray. I liked it very much at St Fagan's.

On Saturday we had a lovely time. In the morning we went to town to see the toy shops. I had a ride in Father Christmas's Our-liner and was given a present of a jig-saw puzzle. We spent the afternoon exploring Caerphilly castle. We had to squeeze in through the railings but even then we could not get far for all the doors to the towers were locked. Then as it was Guy Fawkes' night we had a wonderful time in the evening letting off fireworks and burning the guy on the bonfire.

Will you please write to me soon and if you think of it please send me th

Dear Mrs Jenkins

I must thank you very much for the lovely album. It was very kind of you to send me a present. You have put my last snap in it. It is a very good ladyship. I have put my last snap in the album it is a photograph I took of daddy in the garden keep soft you promised to let me have.

With love
from Roger

With love
Roger.

E-mail: Letter to Horst from New Owner of Greenmeadow, Chris H. Poynton, April 3, 2000

eenmeadow, Llanfedw

Subject: Greenmeadow, Llanfedw
Date: Mon, 3 Apr 2000 11:15:13 +0000 (GMT)
From: "Chris H Poynton" <poynton@cardiff.ac.uk>
To: silvesta@uswest.net

Thankyou for your letter. We are the owners of this house now (since August 1993) and I was most interested to receive information from someone who knew it in 1945.

As you say, there have been many changes, and the house was extensively restored in the mid 1980's.

We have pictures of this restoration process from 1980 which shows a very dilapitated tin roofed building (largely I gather inhabited by animals and a strange man called Bobby Gwyn).

Now the house is restored and we have worked extensively on the grounds surrounding it.

There is no doubt that it must have been a fine house in William Rees day.

We know little about the history of the actual house but quite a lot about Cefn Mably and the history of the area. I am however told that the house in mentioned in the National Library of Wales (in Aberystwyth) and some day I might go and find out more there.

It was probably built around 1650-1660. It must have been there during the Civil War (1645-1650) since a cannon ball was found in the walls when it was restored (currently in posession of a previous owner whom we have met).

After the execution of Charles I, his son the future Charles II (then a teenager) fled to the Netherlands. Oliver Cromwell enticed him back to Scotland and after there ensued the battle of Worcester in 1650 with a severe defeat for Charles. He fled to Ruperra Castle and perhaps even Greenmeadow! Charles eventually escaped to France (probably by boat from Wales). Cefn Mably/Ruperra has, thus always been fiercly.Royalist, and upon restoration to the throne in 1660 (?) it is possible that Charles revisited, or at least endowed the area.

He was not a particularly good king, however.

The later history of the house is currently unknown to me, but there are pictures of picnics in 1901 at Greenmeadow with the Kemys Tynte (Cefn Mably Manor) family.
I believe William Rees was a close friend of theirs.

Cefn Mably burnt down in mysterious circumstances in 1993. It is being restored now.

I would be happy to let you have the detailed history of Cefn Mably (compiled recently by a Canadian called William Jeanes whose Grandmother was a servant there), but would also be most interested to hear about the state of the house in the 1940's. We are most happy there and our three children (aged 12, 9 and 7) love to roam around the woods and streams

Afterword

Gerald A. Fetz

It is my pleasure and honor to write this Afterword for Horst Jarka's fascinating and inspiring book as the representative of one of its two co-publishers, but I am also writing in a different capacity as well: Horst was my senior colleague in German Studies for over two decades at the University of Montana until his retirement; he was in many significant ways my mentor who encouraged and provided wise and generous advice for both my teaching and my scholarly projects; and, most importantly, he has been since 1970, when I joined the faculty some forty-seven years ago, a very close friend.

A few people who have had the privilege of seeing and reading this special book with its surprising and intriguing title while still in manuscript form have suggested that when readers come to the end of this book, *Reflections of Captivity*, they will be more than curious to know "what happened to this young Horst Jarka when, in 1946, almost a year after the war ended in Europe, he was allowed to return home to Vienna, and begin his life anew? What kind of a life did he lead between his repatriation and now, seventy years later, when this book is being published?" Near the end of this book, Horst does provide a few hints about his post-POW life, but he has agreed to allow me to provide a more extensive picture.

Before I start to address those questions, however, I ask for your indulgence in allowing me to reach even farther back than 1946, and say just a few words about his life before the events that are described and illustrated in this book took place. Since I know many of the stories about his life in the pre-war years, through his own telling (he is a spell-binding storyteller) and two written sketches of his childhood and youth I have been lucky enough to read, I can't help but relate at least a few details about his pre-soldier life.

Born in 1925 in Klosterneuburg, just upstream from Vienna on the Danube River, Horst grew up with his older sister and their single, working mother, wandering and inspecting the surrounding hills, fields, river banks, paths, and alleys, where he discovered the many treasures and fascinating characters they held. From very early on, he was an exceptionally curious child, for whom exploring, inquiring, collecting objects large and small, and keeping a journal about his adventures became second nature. Often left alone while his mother worked and his older sister engaged in teenage activities that excluded him, he meandered in and around his home town with its imposing monastery on top of its most prominent hill. As one reads in *Fond Recollections*, he displayed that same penchant for inquisitiveness and exploring in the area surrounding the POW camp at Ruperra Castle. Once he began attending school in Klosterneuburg, he drew the attention of his teachers as an exceptionally intelligent student and, despite the family's challenging financial situation, he was encouraged and received support to attend the local Gymnasium (upper school) when that time came in 1935.

It won't surprise anyone familiar with the circumstances in Austria during the Austro-Fascist period, beginning in 1934, and then after the annexation by Nazi Germany in 1938, that Horst, like most others of his age, was enticed (and pressured) to participate in the Hitler Youth. He was, by his own admission, attracted by the comradeship with other boys his age, and by the hiking, camping, and other outdoor activities that seduced still unformed youngsters "into following" and believing at least some of the propaganda they were bombarded with. Nonetheless, Horst was an excellent student academically, read avidly (at least what he could get his hands on!), became fascinated by theater and music, and expanded his interest as well in the outdoors. He was ultimately allowed to complete his Matura (diploma from the Gymnasium) in 1943. And like most other boys or young men his age, he was immediately called up into the *Wehrmacht*.

However, before his induction, he somehow had three marvelous July weeks to do what he wanted to do. And what did he do? Go on a somewhat unlikely exploring tour (it was, after all, the middle of 1943). He borrowed a bicycle from the Hitler Youth, traveled the first 70 KM with bike and knapsack by train, stepped off, and headed out solo through the "Ostmark", part of the enlarged German Reich, toward the west, staying in hostels, barns, and fields, taking in the sights, and meeting interesting people along the way. He took this trip in part just for the adventure of it (who knew what fate would befall him

once he became a soldier?), but also to visit his Viennese girlfriend who was with the war time camps in southeast Styria and Slovenia, harvesting fruit. His wonderful and colorful journal of this trip, which I have recently read, offers an almost Patrick Leigh Fermor-like account of those travels. But on July 30th he returned to Vienna, said goodbye to his friends, his mother and sister, and joined others drafted into the *Wehrmacht* for training, which took him to what had been Czechoslovakia, the "former" country where his maternal grandparents (Jarka) had come from.

First Austrian Fulbright Students (Jarka with dark shirt in middle row) on way to the U.S. in 1952

Following completion of that training after several months, well into 1944, he was commanded (most fortunately, as it turned out) to join a battalion on the *Western* front in France.

At that point begins the story of the young, handsome "Austrian" soldier, Horst Jarka, whose 17 months in a British POW camp in Wales are the focus of *Fond Recollections of Captivity*.

So, fast forward, what became of that young man when he was released from his Welsh "captivity" and was repatriated in 1946 to his native Austria, which had been restored as a political entity separate from Germany, although occupied by the Allies in similar fashion to what remained of the German Reich following the surrender of the Nazi regime? With his "Matura" (Gymnasium diploma) in hand, he began his studies in both English and German literature, interests that had taken on new life during his time in Wales and that were now destined to be his intellectual and professional focus up to the very present in 2017 at the age of 92.

In 1952 Horst was selected to be in the first group of Austrians to come to the U.S. as Fulbright Scholars, and a new chapter in his life commenced at the University of Minnesota. There he met his future wife, Lois, a bright and attractive American student who later received her Ph.D. at the University of Wisconsin in English literature. At the end of that year, during which he immersed himself in American academic life and in the English (well, *American* English) language, he likely had no idea that he would return in a few years to begin what turned out to be (no surprise) a distinguished university teaching career. Lucky for us, his colleagues, friends, and students here, that career took place at the University of Montana in Missoula. With his now excellent English language proficiency in place (he had obviously followed the often heard recommendation about how best to really learn a language while in a country where it is spoken: (find a girl- or boyfriend), he took a boat back "home" across the Atlantic. Lois followed him half a year later (he was and still is a very charming fellow), and they married in 1953.

In Vienna Horst assumed a position as a teacher of English and German at a commercial school near the Schwarzenbergplatz in the center of town. While teaching, he worked on his doctoral dissertation on the Anglo-Welsh writer Alun Lewis which he successfully defended in 1955. Although Lewis had been killed in World War I, several of Lewis's family members became Horst's life-long friends. After a few years in the commercial school, during which time son Hannes was born (1957), he sought and found what he planned would be a temporary position in the U.S. With a two-year teaching contract in hand, he, Lois, and Hannes headed back across the Atlantic, where Horst took up that position at the University of Montana. Although he fell in love with the Rocky Mountains, he returned to Vienna two years later with his family, now enlarged by one—daughter Käthe had been born in Missoula. But in 1962 he was offered a permanent position at the University of Montana, and he and Lois packed up their family and headed back again to the American West for a very long stay (he and Lois still live in Missoula). And this time, Horst's mother, Maria, joined them.

As a teacher, Horst was exceptional. As a scholar, he became exceptional as well. In fact, he is one of only two UM faculty members ever selected to receive both the Distinguished Teacher and the Distinguished Researcher/Scholar Award from the University. The *teacher* Horst Jarka was dynamic, enthusiastic, imaginative, inspiring, rigorous, yet also funny and fun. Suffice it to say: there was never a dull moment in his classes, whether they were German 101 or an advanced course in the 19th Century German Novella. Horst enlivened the entire German program in a variety of ways, some of which are still, 26 years after his official retirement, legendary. Two stories to illustrate this assertion: each year on Dec. 6th, celebrating a favorite Austrian Christmas custom, a very devilish looking Krampus, brandishing a whip, showed up on campus and in virtually all German classes, where he doled out both candy AND coal to the amused and somewhat non-plussed students. One year Krampus decided to visit the President's office where he scared the daylights out of the receptionist, who had not a clue about who or what this masked, fully costumed devil was.

Student-made Austrian puppets

She immediately phoned campus security to come and take the monster away. As a *teacher*, Horst was always creating new ways to engage his students; legendary as well became his annual course on (usually Austrian) drama that involved the students in reading, studying, and ultimately editing one of the plays that they then produced and performed as puppet plays. These plays were illustrations of Austrian popular culture as it is shared by children, teenagers and adults. In addition, the students created, with the help of Horst, Lo, their children, and his mother—the marvelous puppets themselves, many of which are still on display in their home. It was a wonderful way for his students not only to read, but to bring to life plays by Raimund and Nestroy, Goethe and, one of Horst's major discoveries, Jura Soyfer. Thirty, forty, or even fifty years later, Horst receives mail from students involved in those productions in which they tell him how important and exciting they were for them. I consider myself lucky that I was able to take in several of these productions as a member of the audience in the very impressive puppet theater in the Jarkas' basement on Evans Avenue, one block from campus. Two other memorable courses that Horst created and taught—and he involved other faculty across campus in them, since they were both very interdisciplinary in scope—The Great Depression and The Culture of Tourism. They turned out to be exceptionally large courses, with both students and faculty from a wide range of disciplines. In short: my colleague Horst Jarka was an *exceptional teacher* whose courses inspired hundreds of students, but also whose example inspired a large number of his colleagues across the campus and beyond.

One additional story about Horst's lasting impact on students, colleagues, the Austrian-American Fulbright Program, and the University of Montana in general: In the early 1970s our department began thinking about and initiating annual (quarter and, later, semester long) study abroad programs for our advanced students. Horst suggested we consider Vienna for the "German" program. Only one of us had much experience in Vienna, although virtually all of us had visited the former Habsburg Empire capital on the eastern edge of Western Europe. But after a short discussion, we all said enthusiastically:

"Ja, warum nicht?" The first group of students, accompanied by one of our colleagues, Joan Birch, spent the spring term 1973 in Vienna, and the program was a huge success. We all took turns directing the program, and although there's been what we hope is only a brief hiatus the past couple of years, the program attracted over four decades more than 500 University of Montana students, many of whom went on to major or minor in German Studies. A number of those students, upon graduating, went back to Austria as Fulbright scholars or exchange teachers. We have also hosted one or two teaching assistants from Austria annually through the same program. The lure of Vienna and Austria spread even further than our own program, and before long the Music School was taking one of its choirs there to perform and study for spring term every other year. Recently that program morphed into an Art and Music program that has drawn students from both of those programs and beyond. If there were any need for an illustration of how one person's (Horst's) commitment to creating opportunities for students to travel, study abroad, meet people from different cultures, improve their language proficiency and undergo important life changes, this program has to be just that. And, although I don't think it was really that intentional initially, this program turned all of us in the German Studies program into Austrianists, whether we also continued to teach and write about the other German-speaking countries or not. And our program and university became known as one of the most important "stops" for reading tours by Austrian authors and exhibits on Austrian topics in the country. Through his suggestion, encouragement, constant support, and enthusiasm, Horst and his efforts in this regard changed many, many lives in very positive ways.

As a *scholar*, Horst was also my and several other colleagues' role model and

Horst's teaching days at the University of Montana

cheerleader. When I arrived at UM as a young faculty member still working on my own dissertation, this distinguished older colleague who had played a major part in hiring me immediately showed interest in my teaching and my own scholarly aspirations. At the time he was just about the only faculty member in the large Foreign Languages and Literatures Department who was a serious scholar. And although he certainly didn't eschew non-scholarly, non-academic pastimes and the various ways most faculty at UM enjoyed the marvelous outdoors that surrounded our idyllic campus, he once told me: "you can spend all of your non-teaching time learning how to become an expert fly fisherman (as many of our colleagues have done); *or* you can spend some of that time becoming an active scholar whose research and writing will also enhance that teaching and keep you intellectually connected." I followed his advice and am still, even though I've tried on occasion, a pretty lousy fly fisherman. Because I was interested in a number of topics that also interested Horst, he was always willing to discuss my work with me, and read, and comment on the drafts of my writing. Humane, encouraging, intelligent, critical, and knowledgeable (just like he describes several of the people he met while "in captivity" in Wales), Horst has influenced me as a person, teacher, and scholar in countless ways, just as he has influenced others.

Horst's *scholarly* interests, many of which corresponded to his teaching—writers such as Nestroy, Raimund, Storm and Soyfer as well as literature and culture under fascism—became the basis of extensive research projects and publications. Some interests can be directly traced to his need and desire to deal with his own experiences under the Austro-fascist and Nazi regimes in his youth, as well as his goal of expanding his (and others') knowledge about writers and other cultural figures who stood up against those insidious forces during the years between the late 1920s and the end of the war and beyond. His years-long efforts to chase down the poems and plays of Jura Soyfer, who died in a concentration camp, paid off in spades, for him and for scholars, students, and readers of Austrian literature. Horst's long list of books, authored or edited by him, on this "forgotten" writer from the 1930s have added immensely to our knowledge not only of

Soyfer, but of that difficult historical period as well. Horst's publications on other writers, like the well-known dramatist Ödön von Horváth, whose lives were marked, and sometimes prematurely ended, by the terrible effects of fascism, have been a major contribution to our understanding of those writers and their times.

Even after he retired some 26 years ago from full-time teaching, Horst has remained an active and productive scholar and writer. Two of his most recent volumes, *The Others' Austria. Impressions of American and British Travelers, Vol. One: 1814-1914* and *Volume Two: 1919-2007*, published by Ariadne Press, were labors of love, of literature, travel, and Austria for both Horst and his wife Lois who co-edited both volumes. However, the excerpts they chose were rarely uncritical of Austria. In these two important books, the Jarkas have made available in print a wide breadth of opinions, experiences, and attitudes of "Others," that is, non-Austrians, who traveled, experienced, and wrote about that country during the span of two centuries. This is the 'outsiders' perspective, one that is in some ways a corrective, a broad antidote to the often overly commercialized portrayal of the all-too-sweet picture of Austria pushed by the tourist industry and not infrequently defended by Austrians uninterested in being critical of their homeland and certain times in its (and their) history.

Before I conclude this *Afterword* I want to mention one more important part of Horst's and, later, his family's life that began when he was a child wandering in the woods and fields around Klosterneuburg and that received further impetus when, against all expectations, he was allowed while "in captivity" to spend time doing the same thing in Wales: his and their love of nature and the outdoors. In addition to the many hikes he and all of his family members have taken over the years in

Horst repairing Forest Service fire lookout

Western Montana and its spectacular mountains, they developed a love affair with a remote fire lookout on the border between Montana and Idaho to the southwest of Missoula and the wilderness area surrounding it. As Horst and Lois have told me over time, one of Horst's students in an evening course at the university told him that her father, a famous entomologist, had saved that lookout from destruction by the Forest Service and was using it as a site for his research. He welcomed the Jarka family when they visited him in 1963, and they quickly became keepers of his insect traps and guardians of the lookout. Named by the Forest Service the "Bug Crew," the four Jarkas returned to the Bluenose Lookout for two weeks every August for seventeen years. It was an adventure in and with nature that they all looked forward to as a major highlight of each year, and they still look back upon it with great joy as having been among some of the best times of their lives.

Today, in August 2017, Horst Jarka turned 92 years of age. He remains active, generous, full of good humor, engaged with literature and ideas, and a very good friend to many—former students, former colleagues, neighbors. My wife and I visit with Horst and Lois regularly, eat meals together, tell stories, drink some Austrian wine and Obstler (Austrian schnaps), hunt for Christmas trees in the woods nearby, and have wonderful discussions about everything imaginable. He can't climb the mountain behind their house any more, even though he yearns to do so; but he is still spotted nearly every day walking around the city park close by, stopping only to chat with passersby, friends he has made on his walks. When I see them, they all say: we love to see and talk with that former German professor, that Austrian, that Horst—he knows so much, is so friendly, and has a great sense of humor. "What a Mensch!"

Vienna, Austria in 2006

Above: Lois and Horst in front of the Plague Column (Pestsäule)
Right: Horst and Roger in Town Centre

The Author

CPSIA information can be obtained
at www.ICGtesting.com
Printed in the USA
FSHW020138270419
57621FS